T0129309

I DID IT *Their* ~~(MY)~~ WAY

Betty Lane Holland

BALBOA.PRESS

A DIVISION OF HAY HOUSE

Balboa Press books may be ordered through booksellers or by contacting:

Balboa Press
A Division of Hay House
1663 Liberty Drive
Bloomington, IN 47403
www.balboapress.com.au
1 (877) 407-4847

Print information available on the last page.

ISBN: 978-1-5043-1985-0 (sc)
ISBN: 978-1-5043-1986-7 (e)

Balboa Press rev. date: 11/18/2019

Contents

Foreword

From being refused to train in Sydney simply because I am female to being licensed as a No 1 trainer, (a grading which used to be given to only approximately 30 trainers of the around 1,000 in New South Wales), I trained over 1,000 winners.

I claim that I pioneered the way for women to be racehorse trainers. But did I? After my mother died I found a faded newspaper cutting among her things which described her as the first woman racehorse trainer. There was no date on the cutting but it was before she married as she was referred to as Miss Irene Mutton. I estimate it was in the 1920's. I had vaguely known she had trained horses and won races - all unofficially of course, but as a young kid growing up I had not been interested.

I am credited with many 'firsts', which I have always believed were rightfully mine. Perhaps I had better think again; perhaps my mother, however unofficial it may have been, beat me to being the 'first' lady racehorse trainer long before I was born. Perhaps this gave me the ambition.

More recently when friend Bruce Montgomerie, a retired racing journalist, knew I was writing my biography he presented me with a print out from an old 1927 newspaper telling of a woman riding a track gallop. She was a Mrs. Murrell. At first I thought it to be Violet Murrell, who died trying to save her horse Garryowen in a stable fire in

Melbourne, but then realised it was her sister-in-law, my godmother, Marcia Murrell, who was married to hurdle jockey Harry Murrell. She was a great rider having won high jump contests at Sydney Royal show (as also had my mother), Perhaps, unknowingly, the ambition to follow a horse training career path was in my early childhood influences from these women for whom back then, it was absolutely impossible to do what I did - not because of ability, but because they were born a generation too early.

Please Sirs, I Want To Train Racehorses

Racehorse trainers like other people have dreams. Some achieve their dreams and become legends in the racing world. Some never make it. Very few reach the top. Some, in a few short years, go from being idolised to being forgotten.

I was fortunate. I made it. But I didn't make it by luck. I made it by hard slog, by overcoming the rules which in the 1960's completely excluded women from racing.

I am Betty Lane and I would like to say that I succeeded as a racehorse trainer, doing it 'my way'. But I cannot say that because I had to do it the way the authorities of the time forced me to. I made it from being refused a license to train in Sydney, simply because I am female, to being listed in the top ten of Sydney trainers.

In 1962 the racing world was not male dominated – it was male exclusive!

It was a time that anyone born after 1970 would not understand. Women were excluded from many careers and in racing the exclusion was absolute. Women were supposed to do nice lady-like work - perhaps typists or nurses or school teachers. They could not be trainers; they could not be jockeys, they could not be strappers, they could not be trackwork riders, they could not be bookmakers, they could not even be a member of the Australian Jockey Club (AJC) - a woman's place was to go along on race day in her nice new dress and nice new hat and say, "That's my husband's horse."

I wanted to be a racehorse trainer so, naively, in 1962 I walked into the AJC office on Randwick racecourse and asked a clerk for a trainer's application form. He raised his eyebrows and asked, "Who is it for?"

"Humph," was my only response. But he gave me the form which I took across to a counter and filled it in, then giving it back to him I answered his question, "It's for me."

A few weeks later I was summoned to an interview by the AJC Licensing Committee. Fools walk in where angels fear to tread! I am far from being an angel and although I had no fear of the authorities, I did have awe. I now think I was a bit like the Charles Dickens character, Oliver Twist, naively asking for more, 'Please sirs, I want to be a racehorse trainer.'

I was treated with every courtesy by seven elderly (or so they seemed to me at the time) gentlemen seated behind a large horseshoe shaped table. I call them gentlemen for that is what they were. Their manners were impeccable. All stood as I entered the room and all remained standing until I sat.

"Yes Miss Lane, and why do you wish to be a trainer?"

All gave full attention to my carefully prepared words, peering at me over the tops of their horn rimmed spectacles. But when I had finished putting my case, there was no hesitation, no deliberation. Their spokesman, Bailey Yates, who was the Supervisor of Licensed persons, stood and said, "Thank you Miss Lane; we cannot give you a licence; it is not our policy to license women. Good day."

That was it. No ifs; no buts. As far as they were concerned it was simple - they did NOT license women. Their inflexible decision was final; there was no higher body to appeal to. Anti-discrimination laws were still years off in the future.

As I walked out, they all rose again from their seats. Perfect manners accompanied the perfect dismissal.

I've Made It

F ast forward, 14 years later, to 1976. After being a country racehorse trainer for 14 years and leading trainer (leading 180 males), in the Western Districts Racing Association of New South Wales (WDRA) for three years, an area from Bathurst to Wellington and from Cowra to Mudgee and had trained more than 800 winners, I again applied to train at Randwick. This time they could not refuse me. This time, there was no hesitation, no need for an interview. This time a prompt letter to say I had been approved.

When I went to the AJC office and said, "I've come to pay for my licence," the man attending me said, "Of course, you must be Betty Lane." He turned to a shelf behind him, picked up a manila folder and as he was placing it on the counter he commented, "'Do you realise you are the first woman ever licensed here?"

I smiled and said, "Yes, I believe so," but thought: Realise it? I certainly do, but I doubt you realise the price I have had to pay.

He opened the folder on the counter and looking at the top sheet, raised his eyebrows and said, "Seems you are not only the first woman, but you have also been very honoured; they have given you a No.2 licence without having to go on a Permit first."

In those days racehorse trainers were graded. When first licensed, *'he'* started on a Permit and if *'he'* proved successful, *'he'* could then advance to a No.2 licence, then if really successful, to a No.1 licence. Everything in the rules referred to *'he'*.

No, I didn't feel honoured, but I did feel very pleased. I smiled back and said, "Thank you," inwardly thinking, Given? They have not given me anything! I have earned it. My 13 years of hard slog as a country trainer to prove myself to the authorities had earned me the right to be a fully licensed Randwick trainer; I had overcome the discrimination of that era. I was finally going to train at Randwick and by grading me with a full licence it seemed that the AJC were not only acknowledging my ability, but in a slightly backhanded way were giving an apology for the antiquated rules of the past.

When I had been refused a licence back in 1962, simply because I am female, there had been no equal rights laws; there had been no right of appeal; there had been absolutely no way possible to overcome the AJC's refusal, but now, 1976, times had changed. Now, they could not refuse me as I had achieved what had seemed virtually impossible for a woman in that era. In 1974 I had become the first woman in the world to win an important Trainers Premiership and had repeated it the two following years. In winning three consecutive WDRA trainers' premierships from over 130 trainers, I held all the aces.

I had earned the right to be a Randwick racehorse trainer.

Four years later, in 1982, I was promoted to the prestigous No.1 licence - the first ever for a woman.

Although this grading of trainers has since changed, then there were well over 2,000 licensed trainers in New South Wales, of which only around 30 were graded as a No.1.

Racing – A Male World

Despite being the trailblazer for women racehorse trainers, I am not a feminist. I am an equalist. I was brought up equally with my brother Errol; never told that I could not do something because I was a girl, or that only Errol could do something because he was a boy; brought up to believe that if I didn't succeed that it was my own fault; that I had not put in enough effort.

Growing up I had learned the same valuable lesson many times. I knew that if I wanted something I had to work for it, that I had to keep trying, and in 1962 I wanted something - I wanted to be a racehorse trainer. Submission is not one of my strong characteristics and if I accepted the AJC's ruling that I could not train because I am female - I had not tried hard enough. I knew that to succeed, I had to keep trying.

Racing was a man's world. An entry of a horse owned by a woman was accepted (big deal) but she still could not enter the exclusive 'Members Only' section on a racecourse to watch her horse race. Such sanctified area was for males only! There was a restrictive yellow line painted on the ground beyond which no woman dared put a foot. One feminine toe over the line and a green-coated attendant would pounce.

Racing was on my mother's side of the family. Her father, my grandfather, James Frost Mutton, was a racehorse trainer and she herself a renowned horsewoman. I can vaguely remember being taken to the races at a very young age and being left for short periods to play around the Bandstand area. In those days there was a Bandstand on the lawn in front of the Members' Stand where the band played between races. I believe the bandmaster would keep an eye on me and other youngsters.

We lived in Eurimbla Avenue, Randwick, one mile from my grandfather's home and stables which were in William Street, opposite Randwick racecourse, which is about 200 metres from Centennial Park where my brother and I used to ride our ponies. Fortunately my father was a company director with WD and HO Wills Tobacco Company and although I was growing up on the tail end of the Great Depression of the 1930s when so many families were battling, my brother and I were fortunate in that we each had a pony. Our ponies lived at my grandfather's stables where conversation rarely left the subject of horses and racing. I sometimes wonder about some of the stories, but accept that they were true.

Times were very different from the now equality of the 21st century. One day when I was around 10 or 11 years old, I was riding in Centennial Park with my friend, Cecily McCarten, daughter of the then leading trainer, former leading jockey, Maurice McCarten, and she told me she had ridden to the track that morning with her father. I was amazed. Females were not supposed to go anywhere near the training tracks. Also, I was very envious.

I was captivated by racing from an early age and on Randwick race days I would check the newspaper to see if there was a six furlong (1,200 metres) race and at what time it was on. I would ride to the corner of High street and Wansey road, stand up in the irons on my pony and look over the six feet (two metres) high paling fence to the six furlong (1200 metres) chute on the track. My mother told me I was not to do this, but the attraction was strong and I disobeyed. I was fascinated by the jostling and shoving of the horses; by the yelling of the jockeys (their language no doubt being the reason I was told not to go there), as they were brought into line for the strand barrier start.

In those days it was quite safe to ride on the streets in Randwick. No racehorses were stabled on course and as stables were anywhere up to a few miles away, local residents were accustomed to the clip- clop of racehorses walking to the track each morning and of their walking the streets for exercise in the afternoons. Motor traffic was light and cars would slow down for a horse.

Growing up in Randwick I did all the things which horse mad kids do. Before the Football Stadium was built next to the Sydney Cricket Ground at Moore Park, it had been the Sydney Sports Ground and once a month, on Sundays, a type of gymkhana-cum-number-nine races-cum-sports day was held to raise funds for the charity, Boys Town. There were trotting races, pony races and ladies races, all on a track about three furlongs (600 metres) around. Cecily McCarten and I were 13 or 14 years of age at the time and we would ride our bikes there, then ride in the ladies races. Other people brought their ponies to race and Cecily and I were fairly sought after as we were small and light. Goodness knows how we didn't have falls on the tight dirt track as there were no safety regulations, very simple skull caps, but we, as kids, had no fear and we survived without accident.

Pony clubs were just starting but there were none in my area; instead we would go to gymkhanas held monthly in Centennial Park which were held to raise money for the local ambulance service.

Later as a teenager, practically everything I did was connected with horses. I competed at Sydney Royal Easter show winning in riding and placed in jumping; I was a member of the state's leading polocrosse team, Kuringai; I was one of four friends who in 1960 re-formed the Sydney Hunt Club which had been defunct since the early 1900's - (Helen Carpenter, Judy Amory, Dianne Gould and me); I rode in point-to-point races held by the hunt club; I edited a horse magazine The Australian Horse and Rider for five years until it was bought out by R M Williams (of riding boots and country clothing) and incorporated into his publication Hoofs and Horns which at the time was possibly bigger business than his clothing. I was then New South Wales editor-cum-reporter for Hoofs and Horns for another five years. The last few months of this contract overlapped my move into racehorse training, but I managed it. But my greatest love was the thoroughbred.

At that time the majority of trainers were battlers; few able to make money by running their stable as a business. I had grown up knowing the pitfalls of racehorse training; I knew the hardships, but like the old timers, I had a dream. I dreamed of being a trainer.

However being a racehorse trainer was virtually impossible for a female. It was an era which any woman under 60 years of age would not understand; an era when women got married in their twenties (or younger), had a baby or two or three or more. It was an era when, if a woman worked, she left her job when she married. It was just 'not done' for married women to work.

The position of women in racing is illustrated by a newspaper article and photo which appeared in October 1957 in the Sun Herald of trainer Syd Nicholls' horse, Gay Satin, parading in the enclosure at Randwick. Shock! Horror! The strapper (groom) leading the horse was a girl! Marjorie Downs (known to friends as Widgee) had created history.

Such was the emotion about women in racing that large print headlined the photo: STRAPPER! (The exclamation mark was there.) SURPRISE BY WOMAN AT RANDWICK. It then read: Pretty 22-year-old Marjorie Downs led a two-year-old gelding into the saddling enclosure at Randwick yesterday. Many old-timers raised eyebrows and wondered. It is believed to be the first time a woman 'strapper' has been in charge of a horse in the enclosure.

In 1962 I was a suburban housewife. I had married and was living at Balgowlah where my then husband, Roger Lane, and I owned a printing business. However I still had horses and used to play polocrosse and go hunting with The Sydney Hunt club. I also had a racehorse, Delville Chief, a 16 hands bay gelding which had been leased to me by friend Terry Kelly of Upper Horton in northern New South Wales and was being trained at Randwick by Reg Cook, brother of jockey Billy Cook and uncle of jockey Peter Cook. I used to visit the stables daily, used to groom my horse, lead him up and down the adjacent laneway for afternoon exercise - but no way was I allowed to go to the training tracks.

I was frustrated. Roger Lane was a very decent man who deserved better than I gave him, but I had married too young before realising that the role of suburban housewife was not for me. I had tunnel vision set on being a trainer. So I just walked out of the marriage. Although I had contributed the bulk of finance to establishing our home and business, when I walked out of the marriage I did what I thought was the right thing and transferred it all to him. My money had come from selling a house I owned at Maroubra which my mother had virtually given me. Mum had owned this house with a small mortgage on it and had transferred it to me when I was 18, by my paying out the mortgage with the money I had accumulated over the years, as kids do, from a school bank account and from grandparents' Christmas and birthday present monies and such. I had sold this house to finance our Balgowlah home and printing business.

Possessions could be re-built. I left with only my car, my horse trailer and a few hundred pounds. I left Delville Chief in Reg Cook's care for the next few months.

But it was hard leaving family and friends.

Geurie? Where's Geurie?

S ince it was impossible for me to be a racehorse trainer in Sydney I decided to try the country. I had heard of two women owner-trainers, Dawn Flett, who trained her own horse in the Hunter Valley, and Joyce Wrigley in the West, so as these areas had accepted female owner-trainers I thought they would be the best prospects. There was a glimmer of hope, so I headed west.

It was October 1962, Caulfield Cup day in Melbourne and Coonabarabran Cup day in western New South Wales, when I walked through Coonabarabran racecourse gates and sought the Central Western Districts Racing Association (CWDRA) secretary. When I asked him for a licence application form and by the way he raised his eyebrows, I re-felt the dismissal from the AJC. He stared at me for a while, hesitated, stared at me again, then said, "We have never licensed a woman but there is no rule to stop you putting an application in."

To this day I am still amazed and do not know how or why, but a week later I was informed that a licence had been granted. I have sometimes wondered if someone in their office had mistakenly issued a licence instead of an owner trainer's permit, or perhaps had not looked carefully at the female name 'Betty'. Who cares? I was licensed.

I thought to train at Dubbo which was in the CWDRA area; then the strongest country racing area in New South Wales. However property in Dubbo was out of my financial budget. I had been staying at the Western Star hotel in Dubbo and making it my business to meet as many of the local racing identities as I could. One of these was a farrier, Charlie Cullen, who suggested, "What about Geurie?" Answering his question with a question, I asked, "Where's Geurie?"

A small village in central-west NSW, 380 kilometres west of Sydney on the Mitchell Highway, midway between Dubbo and Wellington, (which would be missed if a person blinked when driving through); population, then, around 250. It had its own 7½ furlongs (1,500 metres) racetrack and although Geurie raced four times a year, nobody was training there; which meant I could virtually have a private training track. But its biggest appeal over Dubbo was the cost of real estate. Knowing the uncertainties of racing and that setting up stables would mean money going out with no confidence of any coming in, I decided that what could not be paid for, would be done without. So Geurie it became.

Another racing identity was jockey Warner Harold Holland, known to all as 'Tiger' who had just returned from Melbourne with a broken knee. Because of increasing weight he had gone there to try hurdle riding to earn money to support his four year old daughter from a failed marriage. I had met Tiger 12 months earlier, introduced for a few minutes by his brother Evan (known generally as Barry and later as 'Rev') who also had a horse at the Reg Cook stables where my horse Delville Chief was being trained.

Tiger had been nicknamed by his family when a baby, and was so accustomed to it that I have seen him not realise he was being spoken to when addressed as Warner. Successful in the western districts until increasing weight became a problem, he had opted for a stint at hurdle riding in Melbourne where the weight scale was heavier than for flat racing. Only a few weeks into his jumping career he had a fall and cracked two vertebrae. He recovered; had another go; had another fall, this time breaking a knee. He told me that as he was packing to return to Dubbo, Melbourne trainer Des McCormick, to whose stable he was attached, kept saying "You will come back, you will come back." Replying, "Yes, yes," Tiger said he was thinking, *'no way, no way,'* and could not leave fast enough.

Tiger, like me, had grown up in Randwick. Also, like me, he had been refused a licence by the AJC.. While still at school at 12 years of age, (but claiming he was 14), he had been riding work on Randwick track for trainer Les O'Rourke but when old enough to be apprenticed he failed the medical test because of a hearing problem which he had had for most of his life. Thus, also like me, he had gone to the western districts where he had been able to be licensed. In 1951 he was apprenticed to JW Blackburn who trained from a property on the Peak Hill road outside Dubbo and on the day he rode his first winner he rode the programme - all five races at Tomingley. He was a boom apprentice until weight became a problem. Hence, his stint in Melbourne because of this weight gain.

Unable to ride because of his broken knee, Tiger offered to help me for a few weeks. It was the start of our partnership from which the 'few weeks' never ended. We later married in 1972 and remained a lifelong team which lasted 46 years until he died in 2008. Meeting Tiger was a fortunate highlight of my life. Not just because of our attraction to each other, but because I gained the bonus of his ability to 'feel' a horse. I think it was due to his poor hearing that he had developed a sense for a horse that was uncannily accurate. In early days at Geurie we rode trackwork together, when, if I rode a horse, and then he rode it, and we had differing opinions - Tiger always seemed to be proven right.

I bought a property in Jennings Street (there were no

street numbers), about one kilometre from the racecourse. I would have preferred to be nearer, but that was the only property available for the sort of money I had. It cost 500 pounds ($1,000). It was two adjoining building blocks, each a half acre. One block had some sheds which were suitable for conversion to stables and a garage; the other block had several fruit trees but no building. But there was nowhere to live.

So back to Sydney where I bought an ancient plywood caravan, hitched it to the tow bar on my station wagon and returned to Geurie.

In a week we had the shed converted to two stables and the garage converted to a bathroom, (that is if it could be called a bathroom), a second-hand bathtub sitting on the concrete floor of the garage surmounted by a wood-chip heater. We fenced the other block into a large play yard for the horses. Thus Geurie, the hamlet I had never ever heard of until I went there, became my home for 14 years.

I made another trip to Sydney to collect Delville Chief from Reg Cook's stables, loaded him on my horse trailer and headed back to Geurie. He was a nice type of horse, by a leading sire of the time Delville Wood, but he had been caught in a wire fence as a yearling which had left a badly scarred and enlarged hind leg. Fortunately there was no lameness.

John Kelly (not the John Kelly renowned thoroughbred breeder of Newhaven Park stud; not the John Kelly international three-day eventer, but John Kelly one of the memorable Kelly brothers clowns at Sydney Royal Easter show during the 1950's and 60's), had arranged for Delville Chief to be leased to me. At the 1962 Sydney show he had told me about a horse which his father, Terry Kelly of Upper Horton, NSW, had bought from a neighbour for 50 pounds ($100), but didn't know what to do with, because of the scarred leg. They were not interested in racing and the scarred leg would prevent him being used as a show hack. When I showed interest, John said "You can have him." So I had leased Delville Chief.

I had a racehorse. I had stables. I had a licence. I was on Cloud Nine.

And then reality set in.

One week later - it was November 1962 - two weeks of heat wave introduced me to the life I had taken on. The caravan gave little protection from over 100 degrees centigrade heat, together with dust storms which lasted two weeks. Accustomed to comfortable Sydney living it was one heck of a shock. Nor was it much fun later when winter came and Geurie gave me another introduction to weather extremes - this time to minus degree frosts which some days lasted until midday. I learned a lot from living at Geurie. I had never seen a frost until then and could not understand why my newly planted magnolia tree started to keel over. That some plants cannot tolerate frost is basic knowledge to many people, but it had not been known by me, a person who until then, had always lived in a frost free area. I also learned what chilblains are.

Some nights, asleep in bed, I would be wakened by drops of water dripping on my face – condensation inside the caravan from the extreme cold. Although horses were indoors with water buckets in their stables, on some mornings the water barrels in the yards were sealed by an inch of ice.

There was an upside to the fact that I had not been well enough financed to buy property closer to the racecourse. There would have been temptation on cold frosty mornings to go straight on to trackwork. But being one kilometre distant there was no choice and horses got their warm-up by walking to the track - no matter what the temperature.

Tiger and I both worked hard under tough conditions. We worked 365 days a year. Christmas day was no different to any other day; horses had to be worked and fed. We worked in heat waves; we worked in frosts; we worked in dust storms; we worked in torrential downpours. We had many pre-dawn starts and many after-dark finishes.

Hooray - A Winner

When I had applied for my licence at Coonabarabran I had been staying in Dubbo and not realised there were different racing zones. Throughout New South Wales there were seven racing zones each with their own administration, their own stipendiary stewards and their own licensing. Dubbo was the border of the Central Western Districts Racing Association (CWDRA) which extended from there to Nyngan, but Geurie, although only 17 miles from Dubbo, was in the Western Districts Racing Association (WDRA) which controlled 22 primary race clubs plus 15 picnic race clubs from Bathurst to Bourke and south to Cowra.

My first ever starter was Delville Chief early in December 1962 at Wellington which was in the WDRA. As I was licensed by a different association to where I had set up stables I thought I had better sort it out with the stipendiary steward in charge. This was Jim Meehan who later became the chief steward in Sydney. "Mr. Meehan, I am Betty Lane. I have a training licence and …," but that was as far as I got. He stopped the rest of what I was about to say with, "Oh no, sorry, we don't license women."

I said, "I am not applying, I already have a licence."

"Oh." He looked at me with an expression of disbelief, looked away, then looked back to me again. But he listened carefully as I explained that I had set up stables in Geurie which was in his Association, but being licensed in the WDRA, I thought the licence should be transferred to his area. He seemed doubtful, asked a few questions, then explained that they had never licensed a female, but, that as I was already licensed that, perhaps, it would be the correct thing to do.

It was not a fairy tale beginning to my training career. The best Delville Chief could do that day was third. At his next start, which was at Dubbo two weeks later, he finished second, and then joy of joys, at his third start he became my first ever winner. It was a Maiden race at Trangie on 12th January 1963. The hardships seemed as nothing. I had trained a winner!

When I got back to normal thinking after the elation of the win, I realised there was not a photographer taking and selling race finish photos as Ron Bickley did in Sydney. But I was fortunate. Somebody told me that an owner of another runner in the race had taken a photo. I found out who it was and although their camera had been amateurishly clicked three lengths before the winning post, I have been forever grateful that they gave me their negative. To this day that photo of Delville Chief's win has pride of place in my office.

This also gave me an idea. For my work with Hoofs & Horns magazine I used to take photos to go with articles and reports - I had all the gear necessary. So I took my camera to the next race meeting. The camera was a Super Speed Graphic, the superior of press cameras of the time, very large, very impressive. Unfortunately Delville Chief's next start was not as impressive as the camera, but I had it focused - just in case. The winning owner saw me with the camera and asked if I was selling race finish photos? Until then I had not thought about it, but the idea of selling photos immediately suggested something I needed - money.

My quick reply was just one word, "Yes."

Although the camera could take photos at 1/1000 of a second, colour film in the 1960's was not fast enough for action shots, so race finish photos had to be taken in black and white, converted to sepia, then hand coloured. Cameras used either negative roll film or slide film which had to be developed in a dark room, so called because that was what it was - the only lighting an orange coloured globe which did not affect film. Digital photography was still in the realms of science fiction.

Besides horses, one of my main interests was art which I had learned as a kid and years of drawing and painting tuition meant colouring race photos and lettering details on the mount were not a problem. Tiger and I partitioned off a section of our garage-cum-bathroom into a dark-room to process film and Tiger's father, Harold Holland, who was a carpenter and who visited occasionally, showed Tiger how to use a mitre box to cut and make photo frames. We were in business.

Another welcome supplementary income besides the race photo business, (there was not much income at this time from racehorse training), was payment for 5,000 words each month from Hoofs & Horns magazine. I was still contracted for another eight months after I moved to Geurie so, to meet my commitment, a few local horse sports got better coverage than they warranted. To make up my quota, I did a series of 'How To' articles in which Tiger and one of the horses became models for photos to go with articles such as 'How to Plait a Horse's Mane', 'How to Load a Horse on a Float', 'How to Bandage'.

Fortunately, photography had more immediate success than Delville Chief, whose second win took four months. The system of advancing through restricted classes of racing was to win a Maiden race, then two Improvers, then two Progressives and then a horse became Open company.

After winning the Maiden race at Trangie, Delville Chief's efforts in Improvers races were getting him nowhere; then it dawned on me that Improvers races had big fields but the next class higher, Progressive, had small fields. Many mediocre horses were able to win a Maiden race but, finding it harder in Improvers class, dropped out of racing before getting to Progressive. So I decided to by-pass Improvers. Good decision. Delville Chief's next start was in a Progressive which he won nicely, followed by a second start in this class for another win. But there the winning streak ended. As an Open company horse, it took several starts before he was able to win another race and then only against a mediocre field at Parkes. This was followed with a dead-heat at Trangie. But he was not really up to Open company, so I returned him to the Kellys at Upper Horton.

A few weeks after Delville Chief's first win I got my first paying client. Local farmer Bruce Parkinson gave me his horse Pickard to train for the coming Picnic circuit, an important annual social event of most country towns. The fact Pickard was to race as a 'grass eater' was unimportant – a real paying client was recognising me and trusting me with his racehorse.

Grass eaters are horses which must be sent to a specified paddock which is nominated and approved by the race club, for four weeks eating only grass, then can go to a trainer for four weeks training prior to their first picnic meeting start.

Pickard's first start was at Dubbo Picnics and luckily he won. Luckily, because with the confidence of this win, Tiger approached Les Gibson who owned Compton Thoroughbred Stud at Narromine. Les, who raced horses in Sydney with good successes, had had his studmaster train a horse named Ousley Lad, simply to support the picnics. It had been unplaced.

When Tiger, who had all the confidence in the world,

fronted up and said, "Betty could improve Ousley Lad", Les told him to put the horse on our float then and there. Obviously it suited him to free his studmaster from the extra chore of training a racehorse.

However, putting Ousley Lad on the float then and there was easier said than done. My one horse trailer had served well in Sydney, but it was just that - a one horse trailer. To Geurie from Dubbo was about 25 minutes, so, while Tiger was taking possession of Ousley Lad, I made it post haste back to Geurie with Pickard; off-loaded him into his stable which had been prepared with feed, hay and water before we left for the races, and in record time, was back to Dubbo to collect my second paying client.

This was the start of a long and successful association with Les Gibson which included, some years later, my first Sydney winner, London Rep.

Early Days

In the 1960's Geurie was a typical country village of around 250 people with services which had remained from horse and cart days. Despite being within easy driving distance of both Dubbo and Wellington there was a post office (with a manually operated telephone exchange - 'number please?'), a one man police station (with a cell in the backyard), a railway station, an Anglican church with a resident rector, a Catholic church to which a visiting priest from Dubbo would come each Sunday for the one weekly Mass, a grocery shop, a primary school and Paxton's Welding Works. Most locals travelled to work either in Dubbo or Wellington, or as farm hands on surrounding properties.

The racecourse had not been used for training within living memory and nobody seemed to care about the condition of the track until a race meeting was due. There was just the one track, (no inside training tracks) of 7½ furlongs (1500 metres) circuit and no such thing as irrigation. In summer it became rock hard so when rain clouds appeared, Tiger and I would borrow a tractor from local farmer David Hall, hook on some harrows and open the ground up a few inches to let rain soak in. Although it did the track a power of good, the local president of the race club, Len Graham, said we should not do it. But neither he, nor anybody else did any track maintenance, so we ignored him - just went ahead and did it.

In summer, if the season was dry, the track was almost devoid of grass; if the season was wet, the grass grew and for a short time we had an 'almost' turf track. Sometimes the growth was too fast and a trainer friend from Wellington, Bill Walker, would bring his motor mower and we would mow a strip about two metres wide from the four furlongs (800 metres) to the winning post for our gallops. But sometimes, in a good season, grass grew faster than we could mow. Then we not only borrowed David Hall's tractor but also his slasher – an implement used to slash crops such as wheat and oats. It didn't leave a nicely mown track, but it served the purpose to lower the grass so we could gallop on it.

When I read in a Sydney newspaper that city trainers were complaining about training tracks being hopelessly below standard, I thought they don't know how lucky they are. Although somewhat envious, I was happy to be licensed; grateful that I had somewhere to train.

Geurie held four race meetings each year which were always popular and well supported by trainers from surrounding areas. Long before I went there, back in 1941, renowned race caller Bert Bryant, gave his first ever race call at Geurie. I have been told that the first race was a Maiden with 16 runners and as there was no broadcasting stand, Bert had to call from the middle of the crowd. Also told that he missed calling the favourite as it got left at the post in a cloud of dust. The dust I can believe, but knowing the width of the track, I find it hard to believe a field of 16.

Our day started at 4am in summer; 6am in winter. In early days when it was just Tiger and me, we mucked out stables, mixed feeds, then saddled up and rode one kilometre to the track, each riding one horse, leading another. There was little traffic, except when crossing the highway, but we had a good view of the road and if anything was coming, we could wait well back. Parallel with the highway was the main western railway line which we had to cross, but trains were no problem as the daily passenger train didn't come through until early afternoon and goods trains were few.

For the first few years we rode trackwork together. Then, as the stable increased and we had staff, I still rode to the track, but lessened off riding work as I needed to be on the ground to clock gallops and be there when a horse pulled up, to gauge its condition. Also, I could depend on Tiger who was brilliant in feeling a horse's ability. Occasionally, on slow mornings, when horses don't actually gallop, but do slower muscle building work, we sometimes took a couple out along dirt roads behind Geurie to give them a variation from the track.

One day, out on a back road, I was riding one, leading another, when suddenly two fully grown kangaroos hopped across the road about two metres in front of us; two bounds and they disappeared into scrub on the other side of the road. The fright I got must have been equally got by the horses, because instead of panicking, as I afterwards thought they would have done, they just propped and stood rock still. Perhaps they had been too shocked to panic. We stood for a moment, then I gave a nudge with my heel and we walked on. It was quite odd. I had not seen kangaroos in the area before; nor did I ever see any again;. That was because I never rode on that road again! I was told that kangaroos came in closer during drought times, which this was.

We had been in Geurie about a year when Tiger's father came for a few months and built the basis of a house for us. He was a tradesman carpenter-cum-builder and soon had foundations, fibro walls and corrugated roof of a small basic one bedroom home with kitchen, living area and a shower room. No lining to the walls, no ceiling, no windows, but no longer having to go to the antiquated chip-heater over the bathtub in the garage! That was as far as the then current finances went towards living accommodation. Knowing the uncertainties of racing I had decided from the beginning that what could not be paid for in cash would be done without.

Some time on, I was training a mare for Les Gibson named Fairy Loch, and brought off a good plunge at Cowra with her. After the win he handed me a brown paper bag and said,"Here put some windows in your house." Inside the paper bag was enough money to do just that. Until Fairy Loch's win, hessian bags had served to seal the windows.

Bit by bit the house was gradually improved and the last thing to finish it would have been lining the walls properly. But this was never done as it had gradually gained a lining of sorts. Having the race finish photo business, it was easy to print off a photo each time we had a winner, frame it and nail it to the wall. These pictures fitted neatly between the studs of the wall frame.

By 1964 I was winning races and the stable was growing and new clients coming along. Finances were improving and I was able to trade in the one-horse trailer for a double-horser. Just 12 months prior I had bought a new Toyota station wagon and although it could pull the two-horse trailer okay, it was really not powerful enough, so I traded it in for a used Pontiac Parisienne which had only done 30,000 something miles. Soon the two-horse trailer also was not enough, so as I had just enough money, I invested in a second hand truck and local welder, Tiger Paxton, built a body on it to carry five horses.

When he had been building the float on the truck, Tiger (my Tiger - not Tiger Paxton) had mentioned that we might get him to make a name sign for our stables and wondered how he thought 'Warbett' would sound - the name a combination of the first half of our names, Warner and Betty. Tiger Paxton must have taken that name as decided and made a horseshoe sign as a 'thank you' to us for giving him the job of fitting out the truck. He made it as a surprise present and installed it when we were not there.

It was in the shape of a large horseshoe about 60 centimetres deep, with the lettering 'WARBETT LODGE founded 1962'. Unfortunately the horseshoe had the opening at the bottom. We liked the sign, we liked the name, but we didn't like the opening being down Bad karma! Luck is believed to fall out if the opening is down - it has to be up to catch luck. But, as it had been a gift, we hesitated to ask him to change it.

However superstition prevailed and after a few weeks we asked him to change it to have the opening at the top. That sign has travelled with Tiger and me and I still have it at my home today.

An advantage of Geurie being midway between the WDRA and the CWDRA was that there were two meetings each Saturday to select from and, now having a truck and a horse trailer, we were able to split the team and go two ways if races were suitable.

Also, we were able to float five horses across to the track each morning, so that by changing them around, all horses were experienced in loading and unloading, and we had no problems loading on race days.

Train Smash

Tiger's brother George lived in Wellington and worked for the railways, travelling by train to Cobar on Monday mornings and returning on Friday evenings on the Bourke to Sydney Mail train.

Tiger usually met this train which stopped at Geurie around 7.30pm for a quick 'hello' to George, who would have left his seat and moved to a doorway, ready to look for Tiger.

But, Friday August 24, 1963, only a few weeks after we moved in to our new partly built house, Tiger was very tired and with race day coming up on the Saturday, had gone to bed early, deciding to give George a miss. We were dozing off when what sounded like a bomb exploding jolted us into full consciousness. In seconds we were out of bed and had rushed outside to see what it was. Although our view was blocked by trees, the sound of hissing steam coming from the railway station gave no doubts - a train crash!

Tiger gasped, "George!" darted back inside, grabbed his dressing gown and slippers and ran.

Quickly, but not with the same speed as Tiger, I dragged on a jumper and jeans over my nightwear, slid into gum boots, which were at the door, and was fast down the street after him.

A few bewildered locals were already at the railway and more arriving out of the darkness. In the gloom the train's engine seemed to be upright against a cement wheat silo - looking like a huge dragon belching out steam. People were walking about aimlessly; nobody, including me, seemed to know what to do. However I did know that photos would be worthwhile, so did a quick about-turn and rushed back home to get my camera.

There was still a snippet of twilight so I took photos on the camera's extreme exposure and slow timing and hoped for the best. Bystanders were not impressed. I got some "tutt-tutts," and, "You should be helping." What help I don't know - the tutt-tutters were doing nothing themselves,

As soon as I had taken photos I went to the post office, one block back from the railway line, into the public phone booth and twirled the handle to connect me to the telephonist. I asked her to put me through to the Sydney Telegraph newspaper. Communication was still almost prehistoric. I had to wait ten minutes to get a line to Sydney, but finally got through and told the newspaper of the drama. There was only one daily plane service from and to Sydney and the person I spoke to said that they would send a reporter up on the next morning's plane, and for me to send my negatives back on that same plane's return trip to Sydney.

Okay, that was organised. Back to the railway to find Tiger.

Where is Tiger?

Fire trucks from Wellington and Dubbo had joined Geurie's own single fire truck and a fleet of ambulances, also from Wellington and Dubbo, were ferrying injured passengers to Dubbo and Wellington hospitals. Fortunately someone had noticed Tiger getting into an ambulance with his brother and had seen it head for Dubbo. So, back home, into the car and I also headed for Dubbo.

Driving into the grounds of Dubbo Base hospital about 9.30pm, the first thing I saw was a nurse holding somebody by the elbow at the top of the front entrance steps. It was Tiger. So I drove directly to the base of the steps and as I got out of the car I heard him protesting, "No, no, no."

Seems the nurse had been saying, "Come on dear, you have to go back to bed. You can't do anything to help. Tell me where your bed is." Tiger, in pyjamas, dressing gown and slippers, hard of hearing and minus dentures, (which were at home on a bedside table), seemed unable to get the message across to the nurse that he was not a hospital patient!

Nineteen passengers were injured in the smash, but unbelievably, nobody was severely hurt. George, like many others, was cut and bruised and remained in hospital for two days. Had he been sitting when the impact came he may not have been hurt, but he had made his way to the doorway on the train, ready to look for Tiger, unfortunately standing up when the impact of the collision came.

We found out afterwards that the accident was caused by a goods train which had moved on to the loop line near Geurie wheat silos, but which had not completely cleared the main line by a few feet (60 millimetres). Although the passenger train had been slowing into the station, the massive impact of the two locomotives jack-knifed the passenger train's engine and three carriages were de-railed. The goods train left the tracks and pushed a hole in the wheat silos.

The Sydney reporter who arrived at Dubbo on that Saturday morning's plane, wrote the report, but it was my photos which made full front page of the next day's Sydney Sunday Telegraph.

What Would A Woman Know About Horses?

In the 1970's, prejudices were slowly changing, but women's acceptance in racing was still many years in the future. A Sydney newspaper article asked how many women racehorse trainers were in New South Wales. It quoted an official from the AJC who said, "Only a few, probably less than five."

In my early training career I had comments relayed back to me, such as, "What would she know about horses? She's a woman," and as if to confirm this opinion, "and she's from Sydney!" To the thinking of the time it was only men born and raised in the country who knew about horses.

What would I know about horses? I knew plenty - but then so do many other people.

I had gone through my teenage years with the diversity of the show ring, polocrosse, hunting and dressage; I had grown up absorbing old timers' remedies for minor ailments; I had written about horses in magazines for ten years; I knew that a horse had to be fit to do its work. When I was playing polocrosse in the early 1960's, our captain-coach, Jack Reilly, emphasized that our ponies had to be fit, so, okay, I got my pony fit - the way I knew - the racehorse way. Pumped him with oats and corn and worked him daily. He was fit alright; so fit that I couldn't control him when we were playing and I was warned that I could be dropped from the team! Seems fitness for a polocrosse pony was not the same as fitness for a racehorse.

What did I know about horses? I knew that if I had horses, they must be cared for. When I was around ten years old I was at my grandparent's home one lunch time where meals were not a sandwich on the run, but sit down at the dining table. Everybody else had been served lunch and were eating, except me, so I asked my grandfather, "Why hasn't Nanna given me any lunch?" He answered my question with his question, "Have you given your pony his lunch?" That lesson stuck.

Although I had grown up thinking I knew what a horse's conformation should be, I queried myself, why are some horses faster than others? When I started training there was little access to the help of pre-sale testing of blood and oxygen capacity as an aid for selecting potentially good gallopers. Conformation and bloodlines were relied on. When still a city slicker I had gone to the big race meetings where the best were racing, my mind intentionally wiped clear of what I thought I knew, of what I had grown up "knowing" wiped of all I had been taught. I looked, and looked, and then looked some more. I looked to check what shape and features were common to the top gallopers; to the horses which were winning consistently. It is said that horses race in all shapes and sizes. They do - they do race in all shapes and sizes; but the less well shaped don't win as often as the better shaped. Many horses lacking good conformation do win, but usually it is against horses with less good points than themselves. Thoroughbreds are born with galloping ability, but some have better blood and oxygen supply and better muscles than others.

Earlier, I said that I trained the way the authorities of the time forced me to. Correction. I trained under the restrictions the authorities forced on me, but I did the actual training of the horses MY way.

I knew how to get a horse fit; however so do most trainers. I think what helped me succeed was knowing that besides conformation, besides fitness, there is a very important third element - that the horse enjoys galloping. Horses are born with a will to win, to run with the mob and a desire to lead. The will to win is not put into a racehorse – more often it is taken out! It is vital that a horse enjoys galloping by having the right early education. By early education I include forestalling anything which will give pain. There is a lot of ignorance and misunderstanding dealt to horses. Horses love to run, but if something hurts they quickly learn to give less effort and, even when there is no longer hurt, they seem to retain an unwillingness to give a full-out effort. If a horse is regarded as wayward I would bet anything that there is either hurt somewhere, or that there has been in the past. Bad behaviour by a horse can usually be traced back to somewhere or something which hurt - maybe overtaxed before muscles were strong enough; maybe joint strain not recognised soon enough; maybe a tender mouth chaffed from the bit; maybe shin soreness; maybe.....who knows? They can't talk to tell us.

Sure I was from Sydney, sure I am female, but I had grown up with an intensity on horses which few country kids had. What would I know about horses? I reckon I knew a lot more than my critics did.

I have never been a gambler. I don't bet. If I did bet, it would be on two-year-olds who love to run; who have not yet learned to give less than an all-out effort. Throughout my lifetime the total amount I have bet on horses would not come to $50. I have had winners and been asked, "Did you back it?" When I answer, "No," the usual come-back is, "Didn't you think it could win?" My stock reply is, "Yes, I did, but they don't always win when I think they can."

Did I write earlier that I knew all about racing? Okay, correction. About horses? Yes. About racing? Not so sure. What I did not know about were some of the rorts and ruses which went on; things which could not possibly happen in racing today. In my first few years of country training I became educated in what, to me, I would previously have thought to be pure Nat Gould fiction.

One thing I learned was that a few devious jockeys were forever coming up with ways to swindle the scales. At one of my very early race meetings I was in the Weighing Area waiting to collect the saddle from Tiger. He was behind two other jockeys, one a young apprentice had his mouth open, the other seemed to be snarling at him. I didn't think much about it until driving home after the races when Tiger told me about it. Seems the apprentice had noticed and pointed out to the senior jockey that he didn't have any stirrup irons on his saddle. The senior jockey had said, "Shut up kid. If you look closely there's no girth or surcingle either." The missing gear was in the trainer's bag at the horse stall, ready to be added to the saddle. I have no idea what happened at weigh-in time after the race, when there would have been a big difference in weights.

Another jockey was known at times to weigh without a saddle - a wire coat hanger giving shape to the towels and saddle cloth over his arm.

In a rort used at a country track which only raced three times a year, there was a row of pegs to the left of the weighing scales on which officials hung their coats. Two jockeys had discovered they could register a lighter weight if they reached very slightly to the left and hung on to a conveniently placed coat. It had to be on the first peg to go unnoticed by the scales official who stood to the right. Seems the clerk-of-the-course, when he arrived for duty, would conveniently hang his coat on this nearest peg and for such 'co-operation', the two jockeys would each put a one pound note in the coat pocket. One race day, when the regular clerk-of-the-course was ill and unable to attend, the hastily found replacement very inconveniently hung his coat on the farthest peg. Big problem. Two overweight jockeys suddenly became indisposed and unable to ride at the meeting.

Another swindle was used in a small mid-western New South Wales town where a local jockey was always battling weight. Before the local race day he would adjust the club's scales to show two pounds (one kilo) less than they should be, then, as scales are periodically checked by the government's Weights and Measures department, he would correct them back on the day after the meeting. Other jockeys, not in the know, were usually pleased on race day to find themselves lighter than expected. For one meeting the local jockey was offered a lightweight ride which he accepted although he knew he could not make the weight, so the night before the meeting he adjusted the scales back three pounds (1.5 kilos); a bigger adjustment than usual. On race day a natural lightweight jockey who knew his own weight told all and sundry that the scales were wrong and ignoring fellow rider's pleas to, "Shut up," he reported to the stewards. There was no way of checking the scales so they remained as they were and the meeting proceeded. But on the following Monday, an official from the Weights and Measures Department was called in and thereafter the weighing area was kept securely locked between race meetings.

I, who, when I first set out to be a country racehorse trainer, had thought I knew all about horses and racing, realised that perhaps the sarcasm of, "What would she know?" had, in one way, been partly true. Okay, I knew about horses, but seems there were a few things I had not known about racing!

Country Tracks

Early days I was grateful to train any horse I was offered, and had to match the standard of horse to the standard of race meeting. Bigger centers like Orange and Bathurst had good tracks and comfortable grandstands, and attracted a reasonably good class of horse, but other centres had less amenities, less prize money, and attracted less gifted horses.

With one such less gifted horse it was not an easy 100 miles trip from Geurie to Rylstone, to race him in their once-a-year race day. It was mid summer and several parts of the road were corrugated dirt raising clouds of dust.

After unloading the horse from the trailer, leading him across to the stalls and tying him up, I bent down to get towels and his fly sheet from the gear bag which I had dropped on the ground beside us, when the horse, normally sensible and calm, gave an almighty lurch forward and knocked me sideways.

My "Whoa, whoa, whoa," suddenly changed to a "Ooha, ooha, ooha," and I too was lurching to get away from an army of ferocioulys attacking hornets.

As nobody trained on the track, the horse stalls had been

unused since the previous year's meeting and, although other amenities may have been checked, obviously the horse stalls had not. A large hornets' nest had grown undisturbed under the corrugated iron roof of this particular stall and they did not take kindly to our invasion of their territory.

I, fortunately was not bitten, but in the short time it took me to untie the horse and rush him out of the stall, he was bitten so badly that he was unfit to race.

Then, early in 1965 we were at a Mudgee meeting where, just before the first race, there was a worried committee. The race caller had not arrived. However the stipendiary steward in charge, Jim Meehan, had a solution. Tiger was there to ride my three runners, but Meehan knew Tiger had been the caller at several picnic race meetings and asked Tiger to forgo his mounts and do the broadcasting instead. Tiger jumped at the invitation; he loved race calling so, no problem - I would get another jockey to replace him.

But there was a complication when there were no spare riders to replace him in two of the races. So Tiger broadcast the first race then rode in the second race, which was called very accurately and very professionally by an unrecognised voice. Tiger called the next two races, then rode in the last which was again called by the mystery voice.

There was only one steward's stand at Mudgee, which served for both stipendiary steward and race caller, and as no different person had been seen going up the stairs before either the second or the last race, the caller's identity was a mystery. Not even the committee knew who it was. When they queried Meehan he told them that it was a person well known to him but he was not at liberty to say. Who was it? It was Jim Meehan himself, who in earlier days, had been a leading race caller in Queensland.

There was also another time when Meehan asked a favour of Tiger, but this was different. There was a horse (not mine), which would not jump from the barriers. When the gates opened it refused to move until the rest of the field had jumped. He would then walk out, trot a few strides before it would start to gallop, by which time it was about 50 metres last. Riders did not have to be declared until on the course on race day and Meehan, knowing how good Tiger was in the barriers, asked him to ride it that day to see if he could get it to jump. He said otherwise, he would have to bar it from future racing.

As the horse was lightly weighted, Tiger said, "I can't possibly ride him I'll be 7lbs. (3 kgs) overweight."

"That's alright, we will allow that Warner." Jim Meehan always called Tiger by his real name of Warner.

Tiger rode the horse and although it was last out, it was only last out by one length.

Renowned for his barrier ability, it was rare for Tiger not to lead out of the barriers. He would give a horse freedom to jump by throwing his hands (and his body) forward as the gates opened, taking all pressure off the horse's mouth. It was a bit risky, because if a horse faltered and threw the rider off balance, the rider had no contact, but at that time all jockeys rode with their feet fully in the stirrups with knees on the saddle - a lot more security than the present day style of tippy-toes in the irons and knees 15 centimetres above the top of the saddle.

Jim Meehan was a very fair man and although he obviously thought well of Tiger, it made no difference one day at another meeting when Tiger's horse jumped in front but also jumped sideways into the path of the horse on his inside costing the other horse six lengths. Meehan gave Tiger a suspension of six weeks. "Six weeks, Warner, for the six lengths you cost him."

At another country track, I was beaten *by* the camera. The stable was growing and we were winning races; some expected wins, some unexpected, and of course, what is familiar in racing, some expected winners turned out to be disappointing losers. One hears of a horse beaten in a photo finish, but who has heard of horse beaten *by* a photo? One such 'loser' of mine was narrowly beaten in a tight photo finish at Wellington. This was one of the first country clubs to install a camera and this was at only their second meeting with the camera in use.

Close finishes are hard to judge. If two horses in stride are fighting out a finish, their heads are bobbing in unison. If they are out of stride, one horse's head is being raised with his nose poking forward as his hooves push off the ground; the other horse's head is being lowered and his chin comes in as his legs come down. Their heads, alternatively in front on each successive stride, is the bob-of-the-head effect which can win or lose a race. This was just such a finish. Without a camera it would quite probably have been declared a dead heat.

My horse was London Rep, a big chestnut with a large white blaze covering most of his face. He was on the rails in this race and, as I was standing in a good position to see the finish, I reckoned he got there. But a photo was called for and the decision went to the outside horse. Correct weight was declared and the meeting proceeded.

Although I had doubts about the result, I accepted it. But it stayed on my mind, so a few hours later, as photos were not then displayed to the public, I went to the office and asked to see the print.

In the photo the outline of my horse's head had a peculiar dished shape, and when a pencil line was drawn to outline the profile, it showed that the white blaze had not shown up in the photo – but it proved he had definitely been the winner by a few centimetres. Early film had nowhere near the fine definition of modern technology.

Win some, lose some. As correct weight had been declared and bets paid, nothing could be done about it.

Wellington, a progressive club had another first around this time. The first to introduce the camera, they were first also to introduce two-year-old racing. When I started training there were no two-year-old races in either the west or central western districts and few trainers had young horses in their stable. A two-year-old, if it raced at all, had to compete against older horses.

I had some smart youngsters, one of them, in 1964, was a two-year-old filly, Terany Star, by Teranyan from Clemy which, as there were no races for her age group, had to race in an Improvers class at Wellington against all ages which she not only won, but equalled the course record. I then had to take to her to Newcastle to get a two-year-old race which proved worthwhile as she won by two lengths from a field of 14 runners in the then race record time of 53.2 seconds.

Armed with the argument of this win, I asked the Wellington race club committeemen to put on a two-year-old race. Oh, no; they thought it would ruin young horses but, after some pestering, agreed to give it a trial.

I had another smart two-year-old filly, Livia, by King of Babylon from Empress of Egypt, who won the inaugural Wellington race and went on to win 15 races. Later, another good filly, Donagold, by Faringdon from Our Gold, who also won the Wellington two-year-old race and went on to total 18 wins including four in Sydney.

Clearly, early racing did not hurt my two-year-olds.

The Wellington two-year-old race continued annually as the opening race of the two-year-old season in the western area, and over the years developed into the important race named The Wellington Boot which attracts Sydney and interstate horses.

Local Staff

Racing stables were a novelty in Geurie. Despite having a racetrack with four race meetings each year, nobody could remember anybody training there before. Understandably the stables attracted local kids to work for us. By employing them to muck out stables, to sweep, to clean gear and such, it released Tiger and me to concentrate on the horses.

Phillip Campbell, known to all as Bomber, was one such local kid. He had not passed the required level to progress to high school in Dubbo, remaining in the local primary school, repeating sixth form until his 14th birthday at which age he was allowed to leave school. Two days after leaving school, he was on our payroll. This was 1966.

At school his hair had always appeared to need cutting (soft red-blonde shoulder length curls, which would be the envy of every woman), but which had brought taunts of 'sheila' from his classmates. But after he had been with us and learned to handle racehorses and started going to race meetings, (and kept his hair cut), he became the envy of the other kids who had mocked him. Then, after he came to Sydney with me as the strapper for Donagold, and she won, and there was a photo in a Sydney newspaper of him holding her in the winner's enclosure at Randwick - whacko for Bomber! No more taunts. He was a local celebrity

Although he learned to ride, he only walked horses to the track and back and for afternoon exercise. He also learned to tack a horse's shoe on if the farrier was not around, and to replace or tighten nails if a shoe was loose. As it can lame a horse if a nail is driven into the quick of a hoof, I would angle the nail and Bomber would drive it through, cut the point off and clinch it down.

When the stable transferred to Sydney in 1976, Bomber had been with us 11 years and he came with us. But, only ever having known village life, he was overawed by the big smoke. He stuck it for two months, then left. A month later, I had a phone call, "Can I come back?" It seemed the appeal of racing was stronger than his awe of Sydney, so we planned for him to catch the train to Sydney the next week.

Here, fate stepped in. Three days later we had another phone call. Bomber had been driving to Trangie races to say goodbye to friends he had made in racing and had been killed instantly in a head on car collision. Both Tiger and I felt it as deeply as if we had lost a family member.

Another local boy who used to hang around the stables, then worked for us when he left school, was Kim Stewart. He was keen and listened to everything Tiger taught him about riding and developed into a good rider; somehow absorbing Tiger's accuracy to feel a horse's potential.

When we transferred to Sydney, Kim stayed in the country, moving to Dubbo and rode as an amateur jockey. Three years later he joined us again at Randwick and, on and off, was with us for many years, sometimes returning to Dubbo for the picnic racing circuit in the winter, sometimes not.

Kim was hopeless with money. He liked a bet and consequently was always broke and on the 'bite'. But he was loyal and he was honest. One day I came home from the races and as I opened the stable gate he almost knocked me over, "Boss, I'm sorry, I'm sorry." He had helped himself to small change I kept in my office, thinking to return it when he collected his winnings from his bet on a 'certainty'. As so often, the 'certainty' was not a certainty and Kim's conscience had him waiting at the gate, nervous and anxious, knowing he had to tell me.

There was one local girl, Kerry Williams, who though not a rider, was as good as any of the boys. She lived three miles out of town on a farm, and came in each day. Kerry also was with us for several years and although she left when we transferred to Randwick, she re-joined us for a short time a few years later.

Another boy who started out with us, came from nearby Dubbo. One morning we had just finished the morning routine of trackwork, cleaning and feeding and were about to go indoors for our own breakfasts when a man walked up the driveway, "Good morning. I'm Spider Webster."

He told us he had recently come from Inverell to settle in Dubbo and didn't know many people; that his wife had become ill and had been buried only a few days earlier in Dubbo cemetery; he said he had a 13 year old son turning 14 in a few weeks who had taken his mother's death very hard. The boy yearned to be a jockey and Spider was hopeful I would apprentice him, thinking that starting his career would help him cope with the loss of his mother.

I invited Spider in for breakfast. At the time I had all the staff we needed, but I must have felt sorry for him and said, "Bring the boy here." Two weeks later a small boy named Patrick started in racing - the same Pat Webster who went on to become a No.1 Randwick trainer.

When I applied for Pat to be apprenticed I was filling in the routine application form on which the trainer was referred to as 'master', and the clerk at the WDRA office said words to the effect, "But master is a man, will I change it to mistress?" I glared at him and said, "Don't you dare." I became Pat's 'master'.

Staff would usually lay on their beds for a few hours after morning work, but Tiger enjoyed erecting and repairing fences, which he often did after finishing morning stable work. Pint sized Pat would often insist he was not tired and would stay with Tiger finding dropped nails or passing a hammer.

Pat's riding kept improving and he was soon ready for Barrier Trial rides in front of a Steward to get approval to ride in races. There was no stipulated number of Trial rides; it depended on the steward's opinion of when a boy (no girls back then) was competent. Trials were often held after the last event at a race meeting; some apprentices passed after a few rides; some had to repeat and repeat; some were never passed.

With two runners at a Mendooran meeting we took both Pat and Bomber, which was unusual as two horses were easily handled by just one strapper and myself. Tiger, when riding, would help unload horses and gear before going to the Jockeys' Room.

This day, when horses had been unloaded and tied up in their stalls and Tiger was about to go the Jockeys' Room, he said to Pat, "Okay kid, come with me." Pat had been approved to ride in races two weeks earlier but we had not told him. An extra pair of silks and boots and skull cap were packed in Tiger's bag for Pat who was quite unaware he was about to make his race riding debut.

The plan to keep Pat from being nervous worked. It was his first race ride; it was his first winner.

From this success, 'first ride – a winner' became a challenge for the stable and fortunately it worked. Over the years, each apprentice having his first race ride, was on a horse with a good chance and they won. A few years later, another of my apprentices, John Sladden, not only won on his first ever race ride, but set a new track record in doing so on Honeycrena at Trundle in 1974. In the same year another rider who was with us, although not an apprentice, was amateur rider Ian McIntyre who, in his first ride at a picnic race meeting, rode his first winner then went on to three wins that day.

Many years later, (with Warbett Lodge then at Randwick), David Smith, after winning at Kembla Grange on his first ride in a race, went one better on his second race ride and won at Canterbury. It likewise worked for two others who were apprenticed at this time, Brodie Chatteris and Lance Donnelly; both first rides were winners. Another Randwick apprentice, Steven Ratten, not only won on his first race ride but set a new course record with Kabul at Gosford in December 1980, and Robert Evans in 1985 won at Kembla Grange on his first race ride on Lord Roxborough (a horse having his first race start), then followed with his second race ride, for a win at Randwick on Rustglow.

Geurie Locals

By 1968 we were settled into life as Geurie residents - but I was not as community minded as Tiger. Although he did not play bowls, he had joined the local bowling club which was directly opposite our place. He was on the local Anglican Church council and had joined the Volunteer Bush Fire brigade.

In summer, if there was a fire, the church bell would be rung and available volunteers would rush to the fire station to board the fire truck. As most men were usually at work in neighbouring towns, Dubbo or Wellington, or working on a farm, Tiger was one of the few Geurie men who were home when the bell rang and he would drop everything, run to the fire station which was close by, hop on the truck and off with other volunteers to fight the fire. Invariably it was an outbreak on a farm.

One Sunday afternoon the bell rang and Tiger, who had been repairing a fence, downed tools and called out to me, "I'm off." He was scurrying down our driveway and as he got to our gate he saw a group of cream trousered, white shirted bowlers, who had come out of the bowling club opposite and were looking down the street to the fire station. Tiger knew them to be farmers, and called out, "Are you coming?" One of them answered, "Not in these clothes; they'll get filthy." As usual, the fire was on a farm.

Tiger did go and fight that fire, but it was the last time he responded to the fire bell.

We now had 14 stables, six of them with yards; we had the half acre yard for horses to enjoy freedom, a large feed room, an oat silo and a high walled round yard.

Some of the stables and yards had been built by local carpenter, Fred Jeffries, when enough cash was available; some by Tiger's father when he visited, and some by Tiger and myself.

A shed which had been on the land originally, was large enough to become a hay shed. We invested in a chaff cutter and cut our own chaff from hay bought from local farmers. Sometimes we did a trade with an owner, if he was a farmer who had grown oats or corn or lucerne. This barter system kept costs down, except in 1968 when western New South Wales had been in three years of drought, and there was no fodder to buy. Farmers were keeping their fodder for their own livestock. That year I twice drove the truck to Wagga to buy loads of chaff and oats.

Fortunately, one owner, Doug Toynton of Wellington, for whom I trained a good horse named Western Ballad, had put down silage 15 years earlier (untouched until this drought) and he was able to keep the stable in lucerne hay until the drought broke.

It was the first time I had experienced drought and it was an eye opener – literally. Driving along the Mitchell highway one morning into Wellington, there was nothing but brown mile after brown mile when a sudden flash of bright emerald green on the side of the road made me do a sudden double-take. It was a patch of lush growth; The only logical explanation was that somebody in a car had stopped, maybe emptied out a thermos and nature had responded to the drink.

Next to our hay shed was a smaller shed which we converted into a farrier's shop and Neville Carpenter, a Sydney farrier friend whom I had known for many years, selected and bought an anvil for us. We had no forge, but the set-up made it easier for Charlie Cullen (the farrier who had first suggested Geurie to me), to shoe horses in a shed-cum-farrier shop where they could be tied up. Charlie lived in Geurie, only two blocks away.

As we did a lot of walking on roads to and from the racetrack the horses were shod with conventional steel shoes then, come race day, Charlie would remove the steel shoes, nail on lightweight aluminium racing plates and do the reverse after the race. If a horse raced frequently this meant many nail holes in the hoof which occasionally caused a horse to lose a shoe. Nowadays, many horses stabled on racecourses are shod with their lightweight racing aluminium plates all the time.

We also had an underground petrol tank installed as we used a lot of fuel, travelling long distances to races, also petrol for general car use as it was not like Sydney where all sorts of goods are available locally. If we needed something as simple as nails or screws it meant at least a 30 miles (48 kilometres) round trip to either Dubbo or Wellington.

I had a vegetable garden which flourished in the rich soil of the area, aided by an unlimited supply of stable manure, and Tiger had a chook pen. He liked fowls and to protect them from foxes had built a fully enclosed mesh pen in the far corner of our big yard. One hen had been sitting on her eggs, just about due to hatch, when a local kid, Billy, came in and smashed the lot!

One of our staff, Bill Leslie, had driven off ten minutes earlier in the truck loaded with horses for Dubbo races and Tiger and I were about to follow in the car when Tiger spotted

Billy. Obviously little Billy must have thought that, as the truck had left, we also had left.

I won't write what Tiger said when he spotted Billy and the smashed eggs.

He grabbed Billy, jostled him into the fowl yard enclosure, and put a chain on the gate. "That poor hen has been sitting there all this time and you did that to her! See how you like sitting there!" Then he said to me, "Come on, let's go to the races."

I was horrified. "You can't do that. Let him out."

Meantime Billy's brother had run home a block away and brought their mother back. Obviously the brother had told her about the eggs. As she walked in, I was demanding to Tiger that he let the boy out. She looked at me, looked at Billy, looked at Tiger, then said, "No leave him there. He deserves it. Off you go to the races."

I couldn't influence either his mother or Tiger, but fortunately the races were only 28 kilometres away at Dubbo and we got home early and let him out. I don't think young Billy was in a hurry to vandalise again.

There were other little boys at race meetings who could also be mischievous, but not in the same harmful way - just impish. Sometimes there would be three or four youngsters who came to the races with their jockey fathers and would play together, not far from the Jockeys' Room. One of them liked to sneak into the Jockeys' Room when riders were on the track and 'borrow' gear to show off to his young friends, quite upsetting jockeys who couldn't work out where their girth or whip or other gear, had disappeared to. At one Wellington meeting an attendant saw a little boy about five years old with green hair leaving the Jockeys' Room with a whip. He tried to grab the youngster, but the little boy was too quick and ran off.

This kid was easily identified later by his hair. It was jockey Harry Williams' son, Danny, whose very fair blonde hair had been tinted green by the effect of hot sun on the chlorinated pool water in his hair when swimming in his local Coonamble council's swimming pool. Danny, who later rode successfully as an amateur rider in the western districts, is now a highly regarded and respectable racehorse trainer at Goulburn in the South East Racing Association who regularly makes trips to Randwick and wins. No doubt he also remembers his childhood pranks.

Another youngster who came to the races with his jockey father and played with the other kids was Rodney Quinn who grew up to be in in the top bracket of Sydney jockeys in the 1980's and 1990's.

Breaking-In

In the cities, racehorses go to professional horse breakers before moving into a trainer's stable and this was the way I had thought it was done everywhere. Not so. In the country, some owners had a mare or two on their farming property which they would send away to a stallion to get in foal. The mare would then foal on the owner's property and the foal would be handled a bit and taught to lead and often that was about all it knew before going to the trainer. Although I believe this was the usual way in my grandfather's time, I had not realised that in the country, some horses still went to trainers, unbroken.

So I adapted (as I had to do with many things) and had carpenter, Fred Jeffries, build a solid round yard, with 2.5cm thick, 2.5 metres high planks - suitably strong for breaking-in.

For about two years we had Bill Leslie working for us who did the breaking-in and did it well, but a few times, before then, when no one else was available, Tiger did the job. Mouthing and education is a specialised skill and fortunately Tiger's horsemanship did a good job on the few which he handled. However, and I hate admitting this, I had one go at breaking-in and the result, while okay, was not as good as it could have been. The horse won a race, but he always pulled hard. I resigned as a horse breaker.

In 1969 two Randwick friends, horse breakers, Harry Meyer and Max Crockett, moved to Mudgee to work for Lloyd Foyster who then owned Gooree Stud. I knew them both well and though, at the time, they were not doing outside work, they did break-in for me. Thereafter all our horses were beautifully mouthed and tractable.

Harry Meyer, the best horse breaker (I prefer to call him horse educator) that I have known and who was at Randwick for many years, had trained Max to be equally expert and I didn't care which one of them did the job. All horses returned from them, beautifully mouthed and mannered.

If a second-hand horse came to me, no matter what its career had been, no matter what idiot had trained it, or ridden it and mucked it up, no matter what bad reputation it came with, if it had been originally mouthed by Harry Meyer, Tiger never hesitated to get straight on it. He said that if it had a Harry Meyer mouth, it was controllable.

London Rep

M y first Sydney winner was one of Les Gibson's horses, London Rep, at a Canterbury Wednesday meeting in 1967. As a yearling he had been listed for Inglis' Easter sales, but withdrawn after galloping around a paddock and whacking his knee on a tractor. Because of this, he was given twelve month's spell for the knee to repair. And then he came to me.

An imposing chestnut over 16 hands, his looks made an impression on me, but nothing like the impression he gave with his first gallop. He had been in the stable about four weeks doing muscle building work, had moved up to pacework and was ready for his first short gallop. So, as we were going to Wellington track one morning to give experience to some other horses, I put him on the float also. I sometimes used Wellington for special gallops as it was a better track than Geurie - only 13 miles away – and gave horses the experience of different surroundings.

When London Rep galloped I could not believe the stopwatch. It showed 21.6 seconds for two furlongs (slightly longer than 400 metres). As Tiger rode him back to me, I said, "I think my watch is wrong."

He looked down to me, "No way. That was the fastest gallop I have ever ridden."

Wow!

But exhilaration was short lived. In fact it only lasted until we got home. When London Rep walked down the ramp off the float, he was lame. I was straight on the phone to my Sydney veterinarian friend, Davies Johnston, who said, "Bring the horse down."

Anxious to know what could be done, early next day I loaded him on the trailer and headed to the Randwick Equine Centre where Davies was in partnership with Percy Sykes.

After x-rays Davies said it was just about hopeless as there was an old slab fracture which was too big to take out and had been done too long ago to screw back in. Obviously the problem had occurred when he hit his knee on the tractor when a yearling. To my very evident disappointment, Davies, (I think in trying to offer some consolation to me), said, "There is only a 100 to one chance. We would have to blister the knee heavily to form scar tissue to support the fracture, then spell him for 12 months."

Tiger on London Rep, me on Western Ballad

Perhaps he thought I would accept the disappointment and take the horse home. Instead, I said, "Go ahead; do it."

Next day, with London Rep swathed from fetlock to elbow in cotton wool and plaster, I was told not to take him off the float until Geurie; that it was extremely important that he only bend the knee to get off the float and into his stable.

About 50 miles (80 kms) from home there was a thump, thump from the trailer. Fortunately we were on a long straight stretch of flat road so I pulled over, got out and checked. Oh, oh! Flat tyre!

The spare tyre from the car doubled as a spare for the horse trailer, but to get to it meant uncoupling the trailer, which would mean unloading London Rep, which would mean much bending of his knee, which I had been told not to do! I was on my own. Big problem.

There was no traffic in sight, but as people do in the country, the first car to come along pulled in behind me. Luckily it was a down to earth practical farmer who somehow wriggled under the coupling, got the spare tyre out, jacked up the trailer (with London Rep still on board) and changed the tyre. I was nearly in tears with gratitude to my saviour and vowed that I would never, ever, drive past anybody with car trouble.

After 12 months spell at his owner's stud, the big chestnut was back in work and showing his ability again. But there was still doubt about his knee, so I thought to give Sydney a go 'first up'.

A few months prior, as he was growing quickly, Pat Webster's apprenticeship had been transferred to Bernie Byrnes at Randwick, hoping to give him an opportunity in Sydney before weight stopped his riding career. So, my recently transferred apprentice was my choice as jockey. Whereas leading Sydney hoops might be not be enthusiastic about taking the ride on an unknown horse trained by some 'unknown sheila' from the bush, I knew Pat would try his heart out for me.

Often a thought-out plunge comes unstuck, but this one went to plan. London Rep's owner, Les Gibson, often let his horses go around without a bet; but if he did bet, he bet well. Backed from 100/1 down to 14's at a Wednesday Canterbury meeting in 1967, as he passed the winning post, the race caller gasped out, "London Rep? I've never, ever heard of him!"

This win went well, but soon afterwards, London Rep's knee gave trouble again and he was retired. I have often been asked, "What is the best galloper you have trained?" I have to answer that I had several horses reasonably close in ability and although London Rep was a long way off being among the most successful, I would rate him in this group.

At the time I also had another good galloper for Les Gibson, a mare, Pahlavi, which though he had bought for a brood mare, decided to give a few starts before going to stud. She had raced in Sydney without being able to show her ability. She could fly over four furlongs (800 metres) but as no such short races are held in the city, it wasn't until she was in country racing that she was able to shine.

A fierce puller, she raced at top speed from her first race stride. There seemed no sense in trying to re-educate her to settle in races; it would have taken a long time and she was to go to stud the following season. And, had re-educating been tried, there was no guarantee she would cooperate. Also, that speed of hers was some speed! So, I used it. There were plenty of very suitable short races on country programmes.

Pahlavi was a great advertisement for me. Among her wins, she set three new track records; one of them a win at Narromine over four furlongs (800 metres), where she made her run from the extreme outside in a field of 13, and not only set a new course record, but an Association record, for the entire CWDRA.

Horse Float or Travelling Cocky's Cage?

One very memorable trip to Sydney (memorable, not because of success, but because of embarrassment), was in 1967. With two horses entered for Randwick, but the horse trailer in Dubbo being repaired and the truck needed for Saturday's country races, how to get two horses to Sydney?

The owner of both horses was a farmer who solved the problem. He had a horse trailer and I could use it to take them to Sydney. Knowing how some farmers' standards are different to mine, and thinking about safety, I was a bit concerned, but he assured me his trailer would do nicely.

Not confident, I asked, "How high are the sides?"

I was told a good six feet (roughly 2 metres). That seemed okay.

"Is there a proper central division?"

"Of course." That also seemed okay.

So plans were made for him to bring the trailer to the

stables early on the morning of when I was to drive the horses to Randwick.

Right on time at six am he pulled up at the front of the stables towing the horse (?) trailer.

Yes, the sides were six feet high - open steel mesh! Yes, there was a division - a single rail! It looked more like an oversized cocky's cage!

The horses had to go to Sydney that day; I had no choice; I had to use this trailer. So, what I called a 'travelling cocky's cage' was coupled to my car.

Luckily both horses were very relaxed and they, myself and strapper, got to Sydney safely.

I was staying at Fred Allsop's stables on Randwick racecourse but, instead of pulling up at his entrance on the corner of High Street and Wansey Road, I drove on another 50 metres to unload out of sight, hoping none of the local racing population would see the bushie's open mesh trailer. It was a Sunday afternoon and very few people about so, as soon as the horses were unloaded, I left my strapper to get them settled into their stables. My one thought was to get the trailer out of sight. I drove a few blocks away to where my parents lived and parked it there.

There was another trip to Sydney which I will never forget; nor, I am sure, will my then apprentice, Peter Stanley, ever forget it. I had travelled to Sydney several times with two horses (on my own trailer), but on this trip we had not left as early as I would have liked, and by the time we reached Mount Victoria it was deep night with no moon, no street lights, only the car's headlights showing the way. As we turned up and into the tightest pinch on Victoria Pass we faced into a battering head wind. Both horses were heavy, both over 16 hands. Their weight and the gale force head wind proved too much even for the powerful V8 motor of my car. We stopped right on the turn of the steepest pinch. We were on a road without side railings, sheer drops on both sides, trees were whipping and cracking, branches flying and it was pitch black. Terrifying!

But there was no choice; there was no option; the horses would have to be unloaded and Peter would have to lead them to the top of the hill.

I visualized the horses in panic, bolting away, falling over the edges. I was terrified, but I had the easier job of driving the car. Peter was the hero. It is hard to imagine how it must have been for him. But he led them safely about 100 metres to the top of the rise where the road joined into civilization with street lights and we were able to reload them. Amazingly the horses had followed him closely - maybe just as scared as us.

Many years later I was told that where we stalled on Mount Victoria, was the steepest section of classified road in New South Wales! With a gradient of 13.3%! Understandably, I have never travelled that road since. All future trips to Sydney were by way of Bells Line of Road..

Peter, a natural light weight, was a top apprentice and went on to become a leading jockey in the west, then later a successful trainer at Orange.

There was another memorable trip to Sydney, not the trip but in the race. It is said that there are 500 ways of getting beaten in a race. Sorry, wrong. There are 501.

A horse I took to Sydney with confidence in my early training days was Henderson. This was in 1969 when after winning seven country races against the best horses in the area, I knew he was up to Sydney standard and entered him for Rosehill. As with London Rep, he was an unknown in city racing, hence the owners were able to back him at long odds and stood to have a big win. Again Pat Webster was the jockey.

Unfortunately, although my judgment of his ability had been right, the result was not. About 80 metres from the winning post - two lengths in front on the rails and increasing his lead with every stride; he had the race shot to pieces when, suddenly, he did what could be likened to a square dance. He shied, faltered, and in two strides went from the inside rail to the centre of the track. The two horses trailing him were able to come up on the inside to get first and second with Henderson third.

The explanation for the impromptu manoeuvre? There was a flock of seagulls resting on the track and as the field came thundering towards them, they took to the air. Well, not the whole flock. One bird was tardy and crashed into Henderson's cheek, terrifying him into a galloping sideways square dance. Pat reckoned it cost him three lengths.

Henderson was a strong thickset bay gelding with an extremely offset parrot mouth which is where the top jaw juts out beyond the lower jaw, his teeth not meeting to grab and grind food. Most horses with parrot mouths find it difficult to graze, some completely unable to, and when stable-fed, need to have all feed heavily crushed. Not so with Henderson; he could crop grass from a mown lawn. The roof of his mouth had calloused and to chew, his bottom jaw closed against this calloused area.

Years later, in 2001, I read of a similar seagull fright when Viscount, ridden by Rodney Quinn, won the Champagne Stakes. Well in front at the rise at Randwick, the startled Viscount did a sudden sideways dart when a flock of seagulls became airborne. Fortunately he was able to get going again in time to win.

Actually, the problem of seagulls is very unusual. At one time, Randwick tried a bleating siren, but it was not effective. Flemington had more success with a natural enemy to most birds – a falcon.

Around the same time when Henderson was racing, I also had a mare, Bally Ann, that would also have been good in Sydney but her owner, Wilf Cooper, wanted to keep her racing locally where his interest was. She won 18 country races including several Cups. However, after she retired and went to stud she produced a foal, Lucky Bally, which I did take to Randwick and won with him. Over the years I trained several horses for Wilf Cooper, all of which he had bred from the one mare. Besides Bally Ann and Lucky Bally there was Kentucky Ann, Swiftly Ann, and Merry Ann who between them won 36 races.

Sydney Visitors

F rom time to time Sydney friends visited. One was Davies 'Davey' Keir Johnston, a veterinary surgeon who worked in partnership with Percy Sykes at Randwick. About once a year, while still a bachelor, Davies would unexpectedly pull up at our front gate with a, "Here I am," with his red cattle dog bitch, Jedda, and a fishing rod.

Incidentally, Davies was best man when Tiger and I married in 1972.

He usually stayed about a week, happily sleeping in the make-do bedroom in our garage. We enjoyed Davies' visits as we not only got a free check over of all horses and he did any work necessary, he was a good cook. While he was with us, we were fed gourmet meals instead of our basic grilled meat and vegies

Once each visit Davies, with Jedda and his fishing rod, would drive three kilometres out to the Macquarie River where he would sit on the river bank, relaxing and day dreaming with his fishing line dangling in the water. He never caught a fish for the simple reason that he never had a hook or bait. Davies did not like killing, not even fish (though he relished eating them). The fishing rod was a guise to stop passers-by being inquisitive.

Davies genuine dislike of killing was brought home to me many years later when I moved into stables at Randwick owned by the AJC and they decided that the dozen or more half wild cats which remained from the previous trainer had to be got rid of before I occupied. Davies was the veterinarian appointed to do the job of euthanizing them. I spoke to him soon after he had done this and his eyes were wet.

On one of his visits to Geurie we had a horse due to be gelded. Up until the 1970's a gelding operation was fairly traumatic for the horse as it had to be done under full anaesthetic and entailed a series of ropes around the horse's rump and legs held by two assistants. As the anaesthetic started to take effect, and as the horse started to sink to the ground, the ropes were pulled, then tied in such a way as to spread and immobilize the horse's legs so that the vet could safely do the operation. The most stressful time was when the horse was coming-to out of the anaesthetic. Most, being still half dazed, would stagger about and possibly fall down once or twice.

As Davies headed to his car to get his operating instruments to geld this horse, he heard me tell two of our strappers that they were to help him and to get the ropes ready. But Davies said, "No, I don't want anybody; less people around, less chance of the horse being upset. Just tie him up in his yard and leave me on my own."

It was the first time we had seen, what was then, a new procedure of gelding a horse. Davies used local anaesthetic, allowing the horse to remain standing, thus drainage by gravity averted the previously frequent problem of swelling.

Somehow word spread around surrounding racing areas about the new technique and I had phone calls wanting to know how they could get this vet. "Sorry. He is back in Sydney."

Another friend, who visited us when he had a chance,

was then leading Sydney jockey, Kevin Langby. He and Tiger had become friends when Tiger had been working for Orange trainer Dick Cornish in the early 1960's and Kevin, then a school kid, used to come to Dick's stables before school to ride work.

Kevin would sometimes drive to Geurie after a Saturday race meeting with his then wife Pattie and young daughter Sharon. One night, quite late, a car pulled up and there he was, eight hours after winning the 1972 Golden Slipper on John's Hope!

At the time Kevin and Pattie bred Chihuahua dogs and sometimes brought one or two with them. They named one pup Donagold after a mare I trained and on which Kevin rode five of her wins.

When they visited us, Sharon would have rides on our stable pony, but as he was too high for a three year old to ride on her own, Kevin sat in the saddle with Sharon half on his lap, half sitting on the pummel of the saddle. Sometimes she sat on by herself, with one of us walking alongside holding her for safety, while someone else led the pony.

About six weeks before Christmas 1969 Kevin was at Geurie and, idly glancing through the Dubbo Liberal newspaper, saw an advertisement for an upcoming horse sale. As Sharon's dream was to have a pony, Kevin asked if we would go to this sale to find a pony for her, to be her Christmas present.

At the sale, held on Dubbo showground, we walked up and down the horse stalls looking for a very small pony. All were too big until we spotted a white 11 hands high pony, which we were told belonged to a family whose children had outgrown him, and that he was foolproof. The foolproof claim is made for practically every pony sold at an auction, so Tiger checked for himself. He sat on the pony bareback, lifting his knees high to get his feet off the ground; rode a few up and downs of the alleyways, trotted a few tight circles, came back and nodded to me. We bid and the pony was ours.

When I said I would go back to Geurie to get the horse

trailer, Tiger said, "Why bother? Put him in the back seat of the car." Tiger wound all windows down, opened the back door, stepped in, and then led the pony in. Being a big car it had enough floor space for the pony to stand. Tiger knelt on the back seat holding him, and I drove.

From the showground through Dubbo streets, neither of us could stop giggling at the sudden jerking about-turned heads as pedestrians did double-takes at the sight of a horse which appeared to be sitting on the back seat of a car, looking out the window. The pony was foolproof and stood quietly all the way to Geurie.

Mid-morning on Boxing Day, when Tiger spotted Kevin's car pulling up at our gate, he put a bridle on the pony and led him around to the back of our house where we had a ramp entrance; led him up and into the house and waited holding him in our living room.

After all the "Hellos, Happy Christmases," Kevin said to Sharon, "I think Father Christmas left a present here for you. He had to bring it here because there is nowhere to keep it at home in Sydney." When she walked in and saw the pony, Sharon froze; her jaw dropped, her eyes popped and she stood immobilized in disbelief for at least a full minute.

Years later Sharon became Sharon Jeffries, a leading horse trainer at Parkes in western New South Wales and mother of jockey Tiffany Jeffries.

An interesting visitor in 1973 was the then Premier of New South Wales, Sir Robert Askin. At least I think he was a visitor. Perhaps he was not.

His office had contacted me, asking if it would be convenient for him to visit the stables while on a pre-election tour of the central west. Naturally I was pleased, and on the appointed day stable staff were grooming horses, sweeping pathways, polishing leads and head collars, dressing themselves in clean jeans and fussing until everything was spic and span.

It was just after midday when three cars pulled up.

Introductions were made and Sir Robert and I had just started making polite conversation when one of the entourage butted in and whispered in Askin's ear. Sudden confusion followed - and I was dropped like a hot potato.

At the time I had no idea what the frantic whispering was about; why there was an unexplained scuttling back into the cars and a rushed departure.

I found out later they had just received word that Harry Jago, the parliamentary member for the safe seat of Gordon, had forgotten to put his nomination in for the upcoming state elections – and as it had now passed the deadline, it meant the seat was being handed, unopposed by the Liberals, to the Labour party.

Hence, I am uncertain if we had a visit from the Premier or not.

Another visitor we occasionally had was Sydney bookmaker Terry Page. He owned a motel in Dubbo and used to drive from Sydney from time to time to check on the motel. Naturally, interested in racing, he sometimes called in to our stables - but we had absolutely no connection in racing whatsoever - purely similar interest.

One day on his way to Dubbo he called in and suggested that Tiger and I come with him in his car to Dubbo for lunch. Sounded good, so we did. Driving along Tiger noticed an "R" on the bonnet of the car and said "This is a nice car; is it a Rover?" The Rover was one of the prestige cars of the time.

The brakes screeched and Terry said, "Get out you mug."

Tiger was dumbfounded, thinking Terry was serious and started to get out! But Terry was only acting and, after stopping for a few seconds, resumed driving – and laughing for nearly five minutes.

The car was his very new, very latest model, gold Rolls Royce!

Female Jockeys

Gradually gaining respect as a trainer, I was winning races, the stable was growing and new clients were coming along. When figures for the 1971-72 WDRA trainers' premiership were published I was listed 7th from 128 registered trainers with 14 wins. I also had 12 winners in the CWDRA and two in Sydney. A long way off being record making, but it was progress.

Female jockeys were also coming on the scene at this time. Trailblazer Pam O'Neill, who had pioneered the way for girls in Queensland, was on a campaign to get interest and support in New South Wales and had convinced Orange Race club to have a race for all female riders. At the time I was still riding track work and was fit, so when I learned about the race I thought, 'You beaut, I'll be in that.' I had the choice of several horses in the stable which I could nominate and I became quite enthusiastic. But when I spoke to chief steward Jim Meehan, to get more details, and told him that I would be riding in the race, he said, "Sorry Betty; no you won't. The race is for amateur riders and as a licensed trainer you are a professional." End of my ambition.

I was gaining acceptance as a horse trainer but had the impression that I was not quite socially acceptable by some of the farming families of the area commonly referred to as 'the squattocracy'. I have wondered what the reaction would have been had they known I was closely related to more than one of them. My grandmother was Rebecca Gardiner, one of the daughters of John Andrew Gardiner of Gobolion Station at Wellington, whom I believe had been regarded as the most prominent landholder in the district in the late 1800's and who had a number of descendants still living in the area.

Although aware of an undercurrent of class distinction, there were others who accepted me with genuine friendship. One, who became a very close friend was Jan Milling, whose husband John had the largest Stock and Station agency in Dubbo. Another was Terry Bootle, who became a stipendiary steward with the WDRA and later the official race judge in Sydney, and whose daughter, Jodi Ann, is my goddaughter. Also Helen and Bruce Sampson of Orange who always invited Tiger and me to their annual Sunday after Orange Cup day 'recovery' pool party, which was one of the social events of the year.

There was one occasion when some locals must have thought me to be a very distinguished person. It was at an Orange race club's black tie dinner on their Cup night. Tiger and I seldom went to such functions but as I had trained the Cup winner that year, we were asked to attend.

When we walked in to the Canoblas Hotel for the function, I was surprised to be greeted by an old friend from the show ring and hunt club days, Les Brown, who had been maître de for Sammy Lee's night club in Sydney for many years. Les had tired of the Sydney fast lane lifestyle and was now in charge of the dining room at the Canoblas Hotel.

Somehow, Les must have sensed how my social standing was regarded by some of the squattocracy, and thought to have some fun. He had developed a night club skill of making a person appear very important and he did just that.

He greeted me in a very loud voice, "Ah, Miss Lane, good evening," accompanied with a very deep, very deferential bow. Then another elaborate bow to Tiger, "Mr Holland, good evening," and as he came up from the bow to Tiger, he swept up an elaborate candelabra from the grand piano at the hotel entrance.

"This way please," with the candelabra flourished high for all to see, he sashayed us to a very prominent table, which like all others in the room had a single candlestick. Les deftly lifted the single candlestick aside, centred the enormous candelabra on our table, at the same time pulling the chair out for me, and with a very loud, "Miss Lane," he gave another deep bow.

We were the centre of attention for the whole room.

No doubt some of the racing crowd knew who we were, and possibly just as amused as us, but as Les kept up his very obvious attentiveness all evening, it was noticeable that there were little smiles and nods as people walked past us, seemingly in respect to our supposed importance.

It was an amusing evening.

Village Lad

In 1974 I had a colt which, bought for only $2,500, had gone from success to success and shown promise that he could hold his own in Sydney. By Village Square, whose progeny were predominantly sprinters, this horse, Village Lad, could both sprint and stay; seemingly getting speed from his sire and staying ability from his dam Conrena. A few years before, I had trained another horse from Conrena, named Honeycrena, for 10 wins over staying distances. Horses that can sprint and stay are rare, but Village Lad could sprint with the best of them and could stay true distances.

After winning four 1,000 metre races as a two-year-old he came back as a three-year-old and won a succession of country Cups which gave me thoughts of the AJC Derby. So in the spring of 1974 I took him to Sydney. He had two starts at Rosehill and won them both; the first over 1,400 metres and the next 2,000 metres, winning both so impressively that Sydney tipsters were forecasting a good showing in the 2,400 metres AJC Derby which was then held during the Spring racing carnival.

After his first Sydney win the Dubbo Liberal newspaper

had an article headlined, "Village Lad breaks local TAB," referring to the Narromine branch of the TAB. Owned by Narromine resident, Doug Oates, local punters had supported the horse and being relatively unknown in Sydney, he had started at the good odds of 16-1. At such odds it meant quite a bit of money had to be paid out locally and the Narromine TAB manageress was quoted as saying, "No really big bets were placed, but money placed by the small punters was enough to break the local TAB bank." She said that when the branch ran out of money at 5pm, they paid by cheque.

When Village Lad backed up two weeks later and won again, this time at 7-1, the Narromine TAB was 'cash ready'.

As in all racing there are plenty of hard luck stories. Kevin Langby had ridden Village Lad in both Sydney wins, but was unavailable for the Derby. We were fortunate in getting another top rider, Ron Quinton, and I think Village Lad could have been right in it at the finish, but when Ron was pulling out to make a run about 200 metres from the post, another horse, Stop The Music, knocked him sideways and completely baulked his run. There was an enquiry and Stop The Music's jockey (would you believe our good friend Kevin Langby?), was given a suspension. Win some, lose some; I am not the first person to have a hard luck story and Village Lad still ran a very creditable fifth. The winner, Taras Bulba was a top horse, that went on to win the Derby, and while taking nothing from him, if Village Lad had been able to make his run, the result could have been interesting.

After this, Village Lad was spelled. Then, back in work again in February 1975, he had a string of firsts - two more Sydney wins, six country Cups and the Invitation Stakes at Cowra's feature meeting of the year. Top Sydney jockeys always attended this Cowra meeting, including Kevin Langby who was back on him for the combination's fifth success.

Village Lad had 16 career wins.

On one of Village Lad's trips to Sydney I planned to impress Sydney racegoers, not only with my good horse but also by the way I presented him. Sometimes when horses were racing I would brush either a 'squares' or 'shark's teeth' pattern on their rump. As a kid I had gone with friend Cecily to her father, Maurice McCarten's stable, where his foreman, a young man named Neville Begg (who went on to became a leading Sydney and Hong Kong trainer), taught me how to brush in these patterns. But, never able to do it as well as I would like, I came up with the idea of cutting a template from lightweight cardboard, placing it on a horse's well brushed rump, and then brushing through the template against the lay of the hair. When the template was lifted, hey presto! There were perfect squares.

A short time after I had come up with this idea, Village Lad was racing in Sydney and I was looking forward to impressing city slickers with my excellent grooming. I still had my ego (dented by my rejection from the AJC), driving me to show I was as good as, (or in my self opinion), better than some, city trainers.

But I was in for a shock (and quite deflated) as there was a girl strapper, only a few horse stalls down from mine, and she had a cut-out template doing exactly the same thing! Seems that as I had taken my template along to country meetings, and quite happily demonstrated to anybody who showed interest, the idea had caught on. Hard to believe how quickly the idea had travelled. A few months later, templates of various designs were being sold in saddlery shops.

Around this time I had another bright (?) idea. To forestall any impression that I was a hick, I worked on thinking metric. Because of racing's public interest, when the government passed the Metric Conversion Act in 1970, racing was one of the first industries to convert. Races which had been in furlongs (1/8 of a mile) changed. A furlong became 200 metres; the Melbourne Cup changed from two miles to 3,200 metres. I assumed (wrongly) that city trainers would straightaway adapt to metric and I made a big effort to think and talk in the new distances.

With two horses entered for Randwick races I was staying at Jim Greenwood's stables on course and after several different people had said, "Uh," or "What," to my metric terminology, I realised my idea of impressing with how up to date I was, had fallen flat. I was about the only trainer talking in metric. So I backslid to furlongs.

Yet, old terms died hard in racing. Now, nearly 50 years later, the former names for distances unknown by a younger generation, the term 'mile' is still used at Randwick.

Betty Lane – House Builder

When I read in the local Wellington paper (Geurie is in the Wellington Shire), that five half-acre blocks of land immediately behind and joining us, were to be auctioned by the local council for unpaid rates, I decided to go to the auction. As the stable success was growing so were finances, so, although having no idea of the value, I thought it quite possible that we could afford to buy.

I was in for a surprise. I certainly could afford to buy. The blocks went so cheaply that I, (or rather Tiger and I in joint ownership) became the new owners. Also there was a block of land on the other side of town, which we used to ride past each morning on the way to the track and on it was an old disused lime kiln with great heaps of lime remaining inside the kiln. All stables use liberal amounts of lime each day to freshen stable floors, so as nobody was bidding for this block, up went my hand. I was the only bidder. We never had to buy lime again; the supply providing more than we could use.

Although we were only two streets back from the Great Western Highway, our property was on the edge of Geurie village and diagonally across the road behind us was a

27acre paddock, also listed for auction. I knew little about the property, but I did know it had a dam and that it was fenced, so when only two bidders were competing at very low bids, up went my hand up again. One bid and we owned a conveniently close-by spelling paddock.

Now owning more land and having a little cash available, it seemed an idea to build a better home and more stables. Tiger's father, who from time to time had helped with advice and help on all our constructions, had died. Fortunately one of the stable clients was a Sydney architect, so I explained how we wanted the house designed and he drew plans for a concrete block house; I applied to Wellington Shire Council for an owner-builder's licence. Also among stable clients were identical twins, Robert and John Hatton of Dubbo, bricklayers by trade, so no need to look any farther for dependable bricklayers. There was a local carpenter, Fred Jeffries. The concrete blocks did not need painting, nor did aluminium window frames, so the small amount of painting I did myself. Meantime Tiger, who enjoyed building fences, was building horse yards on another section of our new land.

The construction of our first small fibro house had been dictated by finances; this one was dictated by climate. By not having walls between kitchen and living area, the house was always warm in cold weather from a slow combustion stove in the kitchen - which was never allowed go out in winter. We had one metre wide eaves, plus roof insulation, which helped keep the house reasonably comfortable in summer. As with the first house it was just one bedroom, but this one had an en-suite. The living area was large and joined to the kitchen area by a breakfast bar and we had a large walk-in pantry.

I would claim that the slow combustion stove was one of the best things ever invented. It was a cooker, a house warmer, an auxiliary hot water service (the pipes ran through it), a garbage disposable (paper, cardboard and any other burnable rubbish) and the guard rail in front of it was an efficient clothes drier. Fuel was no problem as we had a huge heap of off-cuts from timber used in building the house and stables, plus any amount of dried timber from dropped tree branches in the newly purchased paddock.

The house that I built.

Until now, staff had either lived locally, lived in our old caravan, or in the garage which had been sectioned into a bedroom, bathroom and a dark room for photos. Or as one girl, Lyn Mackie, had done, had brought her own caravan. As the stable had grown and more staff were needed, by building the new house for ourselves, the original fibro house which Tiger's father had built, conveniently became staff quarters.

Some staff kept this accommodation clean and tidy; for others hygiene was not a priority. One morning I stepped in to what was now the staff kitchen and saw a frying pan hanging on the wall. I looked at it, looked away, looked back again. Something was odd. How was it hanging? The slot in the end of the handle by which the pan would hang on a hook, was hanging free! Then I saw what kept it there. The pan had a depth of fat and in the fat was an egg slicer with its handle attached to the wall. It was mid-winter and the fat was so solidly set around the egg slicer that it was able to hold the weight of the pan. Not my idea of hygiene; but for the stable hand who hung it there - it certainly was convenience.

Another project on the new land was a swimming channel for the horses. We thought to construct a three metre wide by 20 metres long channel and we would be able to lead horses in and walk along the edge beside them. A contractor started excavating, but after getting down about one metre, he struck a rock shelf and said he would have to blast. That was the end of the swimming pool project. No way. was I going to risk vibration affecting my new house.

The contractor said he would refill the hole, but realising it could be a pit for manure and soiled straw bedding, we left it 'as is'. The hole in the ground was there, so why not make use of it? It never did fill back completely to ground level; although it always appeared level, it conveniently kept compacting down.

On part of the new land we built six more stables each with its own walk-out yard. We still had the half-acre yard for horses to each have their daily half hour's freedom to buck and play as they fancied, but the added small yard off each stable was a freedom few city trained racehorses enjoy.

The 27acre paddock across the road was reasonably fenced, but not well enough to trust the safety of horses let loose, so the matter of re-fencing was put into the 'later-on' basket. Meantime, an owner, who was a farmer, had seen and commented on the large quantity of milk consumed each day by staff and said he would lend us a good milking cow to put in the paddock.

A cow? "Thank you, but no thank you," from me.

"Oh, yes, yes please," from staff.

Three of the six staff assured me they could milk, so a lovely gentle Jersey cow named Mooie, joined our animal population of horses, dog, cat and cockatoos.

Mooie lived across the road in our new 27-acre paddock

and each morning after stables were finished, the milking process would start. It was a circus. None of the three who claimed milking ability, were as capable as claimed. Mooie would be tied up, but as the milking process took far too long, she would become restless, so to keep her happy, we would give her a bucket of oats to munch on. The combination of Jersey cow and a feast of oats every morning produced two-thirds cream to one-third milk!

After four weeks we returned Mooie to her owner.

I've Made It

In 1974 I had 38 winners in the WDRA and headed the premiership from 164 registered trainers. Wow! It was a very proud result as I raced equally in neighbouring CWDRA and had nearly as many wins there also, plus Sydney wins which did not count. The premiership wins may not seem impressive by metropolitan standards, but it was a record for the area, and 11 wins ahead of nearest rival, Reg Priest of Orange, who had been the previous season's leader. There were seldom more than five races on a program; midweek race meetings were a rarity, and as tracks were not Randwick standard, several meetings each year were cancelled due to rain. So it was a good result. This record number of wins stood for 12 years until another woman trainer, Deidre Stein of Bathurst, bettered it.

*Presentation at Kembla Grange race
meeting on my retirement*

First person to congratulate me was Coonamble trainer, John Lundholm, who won the CWDRA premiership as he had done many times. He and I got on well, and on rare occasions if we were asked to train a horse which had been in the other's stable, we phoned each other first. Few trainers were as courteous.

Also that season I had my first treble. It was at Warren with Donagold, Village Lad and Swift Ticket. And another satisfaction during this season was in winning the 1973 Louth Cup with a horse named Sir David. It had been the only Cup in the WDRA and CWDRA I had not claimed - understandable as, until then, I had never raced at Louth, 500 kilometres west of Geurie. Country trainers travel long distances and we regularly raced at Bathurst (110kms), Cowra (90kms), Coonamble (100kms) driving on reasonably flat straight roads, but other courses such as Mudgee, though only a 50 kms drive, had long sections of corrugated dirt roads. Long drives were accepted as part of a country trainer's life, but Louth? Too far. So when Sir David's owner suggested the Louth Cup, I was grateful when Tiger said he would be happy to go and stay overnight. Even more grateful when he came home with the Cup. Distances can be understood when Tiger told me there had been no car park attendant; but there had been a plane park attendant. He said "I counted 27 planes."

A very satisfying result of this premiership win was recognition in Sydney. I believe that records were checked and found that no other woman had won the equivalent here, in New Zealand, England or America, and I was acknowledged at the 1974 Racing Writers' Derby dinner at the AJC Centre, where I was presented with an engraved pewter mug; the presentation speech by AJC chief stipendiary steward Jim Meehan..

Another acknowledgment given each year by the WDRA was at their first meeting each season when races were named for the leading trainers; the winner had the first race named for them, the second race for the runner up, third race for the third placed trainer. The first meeting of the new season, 1974-75 was at Orange, and I was a bit miffed when I looked in the race book and saw that the Betty Lane Handicap was only the third race, not the first race which I felt I was entitled to. Tiger made enquiries and came back laughing. Nearly all country meetings schedule the first race of the day as a Maiden Handicap. Seems whoever set the programme thought it might not be quite nice to name a race as the Betty Lane Maiden!

Around this time Tiger was race riding less and race calling more, averaging 10 to 12 meetings each year, mainly picnics and three or four professional meetings. He was also involved in television at Orange which was one of the first regional TV stations. In 1976 Tony King, then secretary of the CWDRA, hosted a regular Friday evening racing programme, with Tiger as an offsider. Television was in its infancy and the studio was in what looked like a big tin shed, but in a very short time the programme became one of the most popular in the region. Tony, with his extensive knowledge and background of racing, would give a run down on the next day's meeting. It was no surprise when many years later he became chief executive of the AJC.

One of the sponsors for the TV's racing segment was Leyland Motors, distributors of prestige cars at that time, and Tony organised for Tiger to feature in an extensive advertising campaign they had throughout the country areas. (No reflection on Tiger and Tony that Leyland went out of business soon afterwards!)

After being leading trainer in 1974, winners continued and I won the premiership again in 1975, ten wins ahead of second placegetter Reg Priest, who had also been runner-up in the previous season. In his presentation speech after my second leadership, WDRA president, Neville Marks said, "Miss Lane's achievement is not only a great personal effort, but a wonderful advertisement for Women's Lib." No doubt, well intentioned as a compliment, but I was not a Women's Libber. I had no help, nor desired any, from the Women's Liberation movement which was active at the time. I agreed with their intentions, but not their methods. I had not set out to prove anything other than that I was a good racehorse trainer.

But attitude to women in racing was slowly changing, not dramatically, but there was acceptance, and by now, six other women were licensed by the WDRA. Then, for the third consecutive season, the premiership was again mine in 1976 with 33 winners in my own racing association, another heap of winners in neighbouring CWDRA, plus Sydney winners.

I never had a high priced horse; I never had a medium priced horse. I had horses bred by farmers who kept a mare or two as a hobby, or with what would be regarded as bargain basement horses. But, then I guess the horses I was competing against were much the same class. Tiger once asked me, "What would you do if you got a high priced horse?"

Silly question. Exactly the same as with a low priced horse.

I have been asked many times, "What makes a good racehorse trainer?" On this, I have very definite opinions. Number one, is good track work riders. Accurate feed-back is essential, and that is what I had in Tiger. Full credit to his help. He was a wonderful educator of a horse and judge of a horse's ability. Sure, I was boss of how to work, and how to feed, and where to race a horse, but Tiger had a feel for a horse when he rode it. We usually agreed on our opinions of a horse's ability, but at times when my assessment from watching and clocking a horse was different from his (if he rode it), Tiger was usually right. A trainer's job is to get a horse healthy and educated, to spot trouble before it develops and to enter in suitable races. An old adage: 'Keep yourself in the best of company and your horse in the worst', is about the best advice ever given to a would-be trainer.

By now I was the established king-pin (or should it be queen-pin?) in the west. I was sometimes referred to as Tommy Smith the second, at which I would smile politely, but inwardly think, "I am not. I'm Betty Lane the first."

Although I was the top trainer, I regarded myself as a big fish in a little pond. But Sydney was the great big ocean and I wanted to swim in the big ocean. Having taken several horses to Sydney and won with them, and knowing of two other women, Eva Langworthy and Betty Shepherd, who had trained Sydney winners, I felt it time to test the establishment again. Because of the policy against women I had been forced away from home for 14 years, but times were changing. Women were breaking barriers in industry, in business, trade, commerce and sport. There was nothing higher to achieve if I stayed at Geurie. I wanted to return home and home was Randwick. I knew it would be hard to start again. I knew I would have to start again at the beginning. I knew it would be hard to get stables. But I also knew that if I wanted to go higher I had to make the move. So, after winning my third premiership, I did again in 1976 what I had done back in 1962 - I applied for an AJC trainer's license and permission to train at Randwick. I was not the same person who had applied 14 years earlier. I now had the confidence of my successes and knew it would be just about impossible for me to be refused. Apart from my record, I had never been suspended; I had never even been fined.

This time when I filled in the application form the reaction was very different. I was told there was no need for me to be interviewed; that I did not have to start on a permit, which was standard procedure for all new applicants, and that I could train on Randwick track immediately. Finally! Finally! The first ever woman to be a fully licensed trainer at Randwick. Hooray!

Stabling was almost impossible to get in the vicinity of the racecourse as more than 50 years earlier, Randwick City Council had put a complete ban on the building of any new stables. Unfortunately for trainers, if and when privately owned stables came up for sale, they were outbid by developers seeking the larger than average sized building blocks to demolish for home unit developments. Only a handful of trainers owned their own stables; others had no option but to rent from the AJC. But these stables were at a premium and trainers had to wait their turn.

So for 12 months I rented stables from Jack O'Sullivan in Jacques Street, Kingsford, one mile from the track, and each morning floated horses back and forth to the racecourse for their work. Before training, Jack had been a leading Sydney jockey (he was the great mare Flight's jockey), but now, because of a health problem, he had scaled down on the number of horses he trained.

I brought five horses from Geurie and I had six boxes, but I was only there for two weeks and the extra box was occupied. My first new Sydney owner, farrier Tom Browning, gave me his horse Chevalier Park to train. This horse became my first city winner as a Randwick trainer. Soon after this win, one of the horses I had brought to Sydney needed a spell and that box was quickly filled when, on Kevin Langby's recommendation, Stanley Wong, owner of the renowned Tai Yuen restaurants in Sydney's Chinatown and known as 'the King of Chinatown', became another of my new owners with the mare, Wonga Lady. Fortunately she also became a city winner.

When I first transferred to Sydney I had thought to keep Geurie stables functioning. I had good staff and anticipated that with a capable foreman I could race in the country and bring the better prospects to Randwick. Oh no. Impossible. Unheard of. The AJC could not allow such a thing. So I dispersed the Geurie stable of 30 horses and brought five to Sydney with me. Today, satellite stables are common.

A few years after I left, racing regions were changed and some smaller clubs closed. Geurie, which had raced since 1901, was one of them. In my 14 years there, racing had been consistently improving and although the track lacked the facilities of the bigger centres, it had always been popular; the bookmaking ring being one of the strongest in the association. In 1975, one year before I left, Geurie set a district record as the first club to have over 100 starters; five races had been programmed and nine were held with the Maiden split into three divisions. Another honour Geurie holds is that renowned race caller, the late Bert Bryant, called his first race there. Years later, in 2001, Geurie re- birthed as a picnic race club.

Smokey Jack

Fortunately I got off to a great start in Sydney with Smokey Jack, a grey two year old colt that had been bred by owner, Alan O'Brien, on his farm at Wellington. Smokey Jack first came to me at Geurie as a yearling and was one of the horses I brought to Sydney when I moved. I had a lot of success with two-year- olds in the country and rated this horse as being my best two-year-old yet. However as I had not until then raced against Sydney two-year-olds, was I was overrating him? I was not. He was an above average galloper and easily won the first two-year-old race of the season, the important 1977 Breeders Plate by 2½ lengths. Adelaide jockey, Mick Goreham, who was in Sydney at the time rode him. It was my first win of a Black Type race. A few months later Smokey Jack became the first of my six Golden Slipper runners.

Two days before the Slipper, Smokey Jack had a visitor - the 'dragon' from Sydney's Chinatown. The Chinese dragon dance (symbolising supernatural power and bringing good luck), is performed by a team of men walking under a massive dragon costume. It certainly was something different for the stable. I am not sure but I think the visit was organised by Stanley Wong (then known as the King of Sydney's Chinatown), and his son Ronald. Thankfully the performers dispensed with the loud banging of cymbals and drums, which traditionally goes with this performance, and would have terrified the horses, but the leaping and twirling up and down the stable yard for several minutes, of the 10 metre long dragon, had all horses' heads over their doors.

It was an impressive thing for our Chinese friends to do, believing it would generate luck for Smokey Jack in the big race. But luck was not there.

There a million hard luck stories in racing and this was one of them. On the strength of his Breeder's Plate win, Smokey Jack was well regarded in the betting for the big race, but as his trainer (me) was not equally well regarded, I was finding it hard to get a top rider.

An unfamiliar jockey from Queensland had recently come to Sydney to try his luck. I had seen him ride impressively at an Orange meeting a short time before, so booked him for the Slipper. It was a jockey who went on to prove to be one of the best riders of all time - Mick Dittman.

Unfortunately, there was no opportunity for Mick to ride the horse before the race and the first time he ever sat on Smokey Jack's back, was in the enclosure 20 minutes before the Golden Slipper.

As the field rounded the turn into the straight, Smokey Jack was mid field about eight lengths from the leader. Half way up the straight Mick pulled out and made his run and Smokey Jack was flying, gaining huge ground with each stride on the tiring Manikato. On the post he was beaten half a length. One stride past the post he was in front.

"I'm so sorry Betty. If I'd known he was that good I would have hooked him out earlier," were Mick's exact words to me.

So be it. My disappointment was understandable. We were so close to beating Manikato, the horse which went on to greatness, winning 29 races of which 20 were Group wins. But I have always acknowledged that without Mick's ability, Smokey Jack may not have even been second.

Soon after this race it showed up that Smokey Jack had developed a breathing problem. He was operated on and given a long spell, after which he did win again at Randwick, about 18 months later in the Horsley handicap, but he was not the same horse.

Stables on Course

$\sim\!\mathcal{M}\!\sim$

With a stable of only six horses for my first 12 months at Randwick, I had an impressive record of nine Sydney wins and I think this early success helped when AJC stabling became available. I had applied for a stable complex on course and a year after becoming a Randwick trainer I was assigned a block.

Resentment from other trainers was relayed back to me, asking how 'she', who had only been at Randwick for one year, had got stabling ahead of them who had been waiting four and five years? My response - I had been waiting a lot longer than any of them - I had been waiting 14 years.

And yet there was a high price to be paid for these stables. If I wanted them I had to rent and occupy the house that went with the the complex. But I didn't want the house. Tiger and I were now living in our own home which we had bought on our return to Randwick. The property, overlooking the racecourse, was a block of three units; two side by side units, each three bedrooms, fronting Wansey Road and one large unit above which was entered behind from Bradley Street. It was the only property in Wansey road which went through to Bradley Street. We were living in the double width top unit and had rented out the lower units.

This property had a strong racing association. Trainer Frank Dalton had lived in it for many years, renting from the then owner, jockey Darby Munro, who had himself lived next door in another block of units he had also owned. As soon as we transferred to Sydney we had purchased the property from Darby's second wife who, though living in America, had returned to Australia for a short time to settle her real estate.

When we bought it I said, "I'll live here till the day I die." Twelve months later we moved out.

The complex offered to me by the AJC had been those of trainer Frank McGrath senior, 158 Doncaster Ave, Kensington, from where he had trained dual Melbourne Cup winner Peter Pan. Between his home, a large Victorian terrace, and his stables, had been a vacant block and on this his son Frank McGrath junior had built a house for his young family when he took over training from his father in 1946. When he retired, the AJC had bought the house and stables and rented them to trainer Arthur 'Skeeter' Bentley who had recently died. Hence they were being offered to me.

I was happy to pay the rent and suggested to put our staff in the house, but the AJC said it was too good for staff. Actually it was a nice home and the whole set-up was ideal: 20 boxes, two yards, feed room, tack room, two sand rolls, a huge loft, a foreman's unit and staff rooms. The front entrance was from the street; the back entrance directly to the racecourse. If I had refused the house, there were dozens of other trainers who would have jumped at the chance to have the complex. Stabling was in great demand and the AJC had a long list of applicants.

I had to choose my priorities. Stables were essential; my home was not.

Perhaps I should have gone back to the AJC and told them that we had our own home; perhaps they may have given me a different block of stables. But I was not game to risk being thought ungrateful with the possibility of never offered stables again. I had battled to get this far, and no way was I going to be stopped now.

So we sadly sold the Wansey Road property and moved into the AJC's house at 158 Doncaster Avenue, Kensington, but I was never happy living there, disappointed at leaving what I had thought would be home for the rest of my life.

The only consolation was that Davies Johnson and his wife Wendy bought the Wansey road real estate from us. They were living in their Botany street, Randwick home, a charming 19th century two storey stone cottage just 100 metres from his veterinary practice, Randwick Equine centre where Davies was in partnership with Percy Sykes. I was surprised that they would leave that home, but they obviously liked the Wansey Road home as much as Tiger and I did.

After being restricted to six horses at Jack O'Sullivan's stables, I now had 22 boxes, but these were soon filled. Along with getting the stables I gained a bonus when Malcolm Rich, who had been one of Skeeter Bentley's clients, left four horses with me. It was not until many years later when I read Bill Waterhouse's book, "What Are The Odds", that I realised Malcom Rich was one of Sydney's biggest punters! I had no idea. His horses though not outstanding were useful and in winning races, added to my success average - which I think helped me being promoted to a No1 trainer's licence a few years later.

I also inherited a cat from Skeeter's widow. Their pet dog had lived in the house and their white Persian cat, Cookie, had lived in the stables. Dog and cat were bitter enemies and woe-betide if one went into the other's territory. Understandably, it would have been difficult for her to take them to live together in her new home. There was however another cat which had to be considered. It had wandered in to Jack O' Sullivan's stables and as I had been feeding it, I had thought to bring with me to the new stables. Fortunately Jack said that cat could stay with him at the stables it knew, and thus Bentley's cat could stay undisrupted at the stables which it knew. Problem solved.

Then one of Skeeter's stable hands who had lived at the stables caused problems for me. He wanted to leave his two very large dogs at the stables. This was a very different matter; and would not have been workable. I had my own cattle dog who would not have taken kindly to other dogs.

Next thing, a very incorrect article came out in a Sydney newspaper seeking a home for Skeeter Bentley's dogs. The article said that with Skeeter's death there was nobody to care for them as Betty Lane would not allow them to remain at the stables! The article was completely wrong. They were NOT Skeeter's dogs! The stable hand was being blatantly opportunist. This very incorrect article was quite damaging.

As I no longer rode track work and as it was nearly a one kilometre walk from the stables to the centre of the course from where I supervised training, I needed transport. On the racecourse transport is four-legged. I had given our Geurie pony to a teenage girl in Dubbo for a good home when limited to six horse boxes at Jack O'Sullivan's stables and could hardly ask for him back, so I went to a Parramatta horse sale to buy a pony.

My transport at trackwork, pony Ickle

The stables were full, so the need was for a small pony that wouldn't take up a box. There was a vacant area in the yard, well protected, which only needed a roof to make it comfortable, and in front of it was space enough to fence into a small walk-out yard. The only place to get a pony quickly was the monthly Parramatta Horse Sales so I went. I was looking for a pony about 13.2 hands but there was nothing there. There were a few bigger ponies which seemed suitable, but a bigger pony would have been cramped in the makeshift stable. There was only one pony which seemed remotely suitable - a 12.2 hands piebald. Not what I was after, but he was thick set and seemed strong. I didn't fancy another trip to Parramatta, so I bought him.

Named Ickle (by an owner's small daughter who couldn't yet say "little" properly), he became a great asset to the stable. Not only my taxi around the course, he was an outstanding lead pony. Possibly because he was so short, he was able to ram himself under a racehorse's elbow and push it anywhere I wanted. All racehorses responded to him far better than I had ever had with bigger ponies. He would never flinch away from a racehorse being led, and would push the horse where I wanted it to go.

I hadn't given thought to him being a piebald when I bought him. To me, a horse's colour didn't matter. I wouldn't care if a horse was pink with purple spots, provided it could do its job. But Ickle's size and colouring did concern a few racehorses the first time they spotted him. Most took no notice, but a few newcomer horses could be recognised as having their first morning on the track by their 'double-take' when they spotted him. Had I realised that his colouring might upset some horses I would not have bought him. But it only happened very occasionally to a few, and only on their first day sighting. Thereafter horses were unconcerned.

Two Year Olds

A horse in the stable at this time was the brilliant galloper, Moabite - but I never got a chance to race her. Rails bookmaker, Jack Muir phoned me in 1977 about training a filly he had bred from his mare Lady Clare. He had raced horses previously with other trainers, but none for over ten years. I was a little uneasy about training for a bookmaker, but I had known his wife, then Vida Dalzeil, back in my pre-training days when we competed at shows and hunting together, and could see no reason not to train for him. He asked me to contact the stud where the filly was and make arrangements to have her broken in. I phoned the stud but they were surprised - she was only a weanling. So, when I phoned Jack and told him that he must have been mixed up with her age, he said to do as I thought, when I thought, just let him know when it was time for her to race.

I waited until she was a yearling, then in mid 1978 arranged for her to come to the stables. Ron 'Gogo' Fitzsimmons, a horse breaker who was working for me at the time, broke her in at the stables. I contacted Jack Muir to let him know the progress, but he only once came to see her, and again said to do whatever I thought; just let him know when she was ready.

We taught her to work with other horses and to jump from the barriers, but one thing she did not have to be taught was how to gallop. She was a natural.

Jack did come to the official two-year-old barrier trials held in September at Randwick where she blitzed them. I told him she was special, that she was Golden Slipper material, that she was just as good, if not better than, Smokey Jack, who had run 2nd in the 1978 Slipper and as a time table for a Golden Slipper preparation I would like to now give her a spell. I also told him she had a capped hock but it was not troubling her and would probably go down during the spell. A capped hock, which is not uncommon, is a soft ball of fluid on the hock, usually caused by bumping the stable wall or bumping in a float and is not regarded as an unsoundness. Horses can race with a capped hock and it doesn't affect them.

She went for the spell as I suggested, but she never came back. Possibly, if I had just said that she might win a race or two, and had not mentioned the capped hock, I might have kept her. I was told later that Jack had thought I was 'con'ing him about how good she was and about being Golden Slipper material. I assume he thought I was keeping something from him and that he had also not believed me that the hock was not a problem.

I had nominated her for the Slipper, but from the spell she went to Grahame Begg's stable. At the time of Slipper acceptances, Grahame obviously had not realised her ability and he did not accept. When he did start her, she won her first start, then her second start, third, fourth, fifth – unbeaten! Five wins straight against top Sydney horses!

And Jack Muir thought I was 'con'ing' him! Huh!

Although I missed out on Moabite, I had other good horses in the stable at this time. One was Jumpin' Pin who set a record for the Randwick track over 1800 metres (which still stands at time of writing).

Another was a two-year-old that had the quality to be a 1980 Golden Slipper qualifier - a two-year-old with brilliant speed named Kabul. By Marrakesh from Mystic Vale, he was lightly framed and only 15 hands high, and on first sight gave no impression of what was to come. But as soon as he stepped on the track it was a different matter. This horse's potential was geatly brought out by Tiger who put his heart into educating him as a 'thank you' to his owner, Dr. Alex Gorshenin, an ear, nose and throat specialist who was instrumental in the then partially-deaf Tiger, regaining his hearing.

Alex had raced Kabul's sire, Marrakesh, in the 1970's and it was his dream to breed a good horse. He had bought eight brood mares, but with the first crop of foals he had become disenchanted and sold all, except Kabul and one filly.

My stables were three doors away from trainer Brian Mayfield Smith, who had transferred to Randwick from Queensland in 1976 and was renting stables from retired trainer Fil Allotta. When, in 1978, Brian gained the position of trainer at Stan and Millie Fox's large private stable, Nebo Lodge, at Rosehill, his clients were looking for a new trainer. One of these was Alex Gorshenin, and Brian recommended me.

I took over Alex's mare, Pepway, from Brian and, when I won a race at Randwick with her, Alex sent me Kabul – a yearling, just broken in.

After training for Alex for a few months we discussed Tiger's hearing (or rather lack of hearing), and he suggested a visit to his rooms in Macquarie Street in Sydney. I went with Tiger, and after various questions and tests, Alex said that not much could be done, and to give thought to a hearing aid.

Knowing what Tiger's reaction to the thought of a hearing aid would be, I asked, "What would you do if it was your hearing?" He seemed to ponder for a bit, then replied, "I'd go to America. There's a doctor in Los Angeles, Jim Sheehy, who is the best in the world, and who has a new technique." I said, "Right. Can Tiger go?"

He gave me a surprised look; but no answer. He seemed to be thinking and didn't answer for quite some time, then, "Why not? In fact I'll go with him; I'll arrange it; I want to learn this new technique."

Tiger, who was already riding Kabul in all its track work, put his heart into the horse, determined, as a 'thank you' to Alex, that the horse be perfectly educated. All went to plan and Kabul won the Tiny Tots Stakes at Rosehill in October 1979.

Tiger and Alex went to Los Angeles together, where, thanks to Alex's influence, the fully booked Jim Sheehy had fitted Tiger in for an operation on Christmas Eve 1979. The procedure was to be in two stages for each ear. On this, his first trip, all bones were removed from his right ear and he was booked to go back to America again in six months to have a prosthesis inserted.

A week after they flew home from America in January 1980, Tiger wanted to ride Kabul's final gallop before the Sunnyside Handicap at Randwick. But he had come home with instructions that his ear was not to be knocked nor his head jerked, so riding work was absolutely forbidden. However, Tiger's education was there and Kabul won the Sunnyside easily, which together with another win at Gosford, qualified him as a starter in the 1980 Golden Slipper. Although unplaced in the Slipper he ran a good race and Alex said it was his greatest thrill.

There was however, a sideline win for the stable. It was the first year the AJC awarded a prize ($250), to the strapper with the best presented horse and Kabul and his strapper, Joanne Clark won it.

Kabul went on to win five races

Six months after his first ear operation, Tiger went to America by himself for the prosthesis insertion but when his third trip was due to have the left ear bones removed, Alex travelled with him again. They had become good friends. Then, another six months on, the time his left ear prosthesis was due to be inserted, the operation was being done in Sydney and it so happened that I was also training for another Macquarie Street ear, nose and throat specialist, surgeon John Walker. Hence, no need for a fourth trip; John did the operation at St Vincent's hospital. All this happened before cochlear implants were available in Australia. Subsequently I read in a Reader's Digest magazine of a marvellous 'new' operation to restore hearing which described Tiger's operations which had been done three years earlier!

His hearing was now perfect and remained so until he died. Any wonder he had put his heart into educating Alex's horse. Tiger joked that there was a downside to his good hearing - that he lost his ability to lip read. Previously, when race riding, when rival trainers were giving riding instructions to their jockeys, he, by lip reading, knew what the opposition's tactics were going to be. It was soon after this, in 1981, that Tiger then aged 44, turned in his jockey's licence and registered as stable foreman.

It was also in that year that another good two year old entered the stable, a filly that went on to become Sydney's top Two Year Old filly of the Year.

In 1981 had a phone call from Diane Lanham, a successful private breeder at Glossodia, near Wilberforce, saying she had two yearling fillies and if I had any clients who might be interested in leasing. One was by Baguette, the other by Duke Ellington. Had it only been a filly by Duke Ellington, I would have thanked her, but not been interested. However the Baguette breed were winning plenty of races, so I said "Yes," and drove out to her property to see her Baguette filly.

When I saw the strong chestnut Duke Ellington filly I didn't hesitate, "I'll have them both."

*Warren Saunders, John Fleming, Dave
Robinson, strapper Lance Donnelly, Laurie
Doust and Doug Fleming with Belle Tetue
after her Gimcrack Stakes win.*

At the time. I had just won a race at Randwick with a filly, Peaceful Princess, that I was training for Ernie Cochrane and five of his friends who were administrators of the St George Rugby League club: Laurie Doust, Dave Robinson, John Fleming, Doug Fleming and Warren Saunders. Ernie, in partnership with his father Ted, had been a successful owner for many years in Sydney racing, but Peaceful Princess had been his first winner in my Randwick stable - and the first ever win for the St. George group.

Back in 1975 at Geurie, I had trained a horse named Bus Stop for Ernie. This horse had been in Tom Smith's stable but, after several Sydney starts, was still a Maiden. He came to me from a spell and after two month's work he bolted in at Wellington, his first start for me, by nine lengths I was acclaimed as having improved the horse, but not so. I take credit for getting him fit, but he had been well educated by Smith and was racing against an easier field than Sydney class. Bus Stop won several more races for me and it was because of these successes which had impressed Ernie, that he asked me to train for him now that I was a Randwick trainer.

It seems that after Peaceful Princess' Randwick win, the St George group became keener and wanted to lease another horse. So I suggested the Duke Ellington filly. She was named Belle Tetue and developed in to Sydney's top two year old filly of that season. The Baguette filly, Allegresse, though a winner, never amounted to the same success.

Belle Tetue bolted in to win the first race of the 1982 two-year-old season, the Gimcrack Stakes in October at Randwick by 5½ lengths. After this win I set her for the Maribyrnong Plate at Flemington.

Booked on a plane for a night flight to Melbourne, she travelled quietly on the float to Mascot airport. A strong-willed filly, if things were not to her liking she would not cooperate. Seemingly the disruption of her normal night time routine was not to her liking. Nor were the unaccustomed surroundings of the airport, the tarmac, and the plane. She put on a rodeo act and absolutely refused to load on the plane. Instead she had to be loaded back on the float and returned to stables. She then left next day on a two day trip to Melbourne by road. Despite this unscheduled tiring trip, she was still able to run a great 2nd in the Maribyrnong Plate.

Later on, I was asked to nominate her for Caulfield's 1200 metre Blue Diamond, a race that would have been ideal. It was tempting, but I chose to by-pass another exhausting road trip to Melbourne; it was too close to the 1983 Golden Slipper for which she was already qualified. In the Slipper she ran a close fourth.

Belle Tetue developed into of Sydney's most consistent gallopers and was rated the top two year old filly of the year. Her success was illustrated when, after a win at Warwick Farm in 1984, a newspaper article was headlined 'BELLE JOINS THE CLUB'. The so-called 'club' was of horses that had won over $100,000 in prize money. It may not seem much by today's values, but in the 1980's this was big money which very few horses reached.

At the time of the article her $100,000 prize money was made up by wins in the Gimcrack Stakes, the Indian Summer Handicap, Luddenham Handicap, Leslie Rouse Handicap and seconds in the Sires' Produce Stakes, VRC Maribyrnong Plate, the Silver Slipper, and fourth in the Golden Slipper.

After this newspaper article she continued on and added another four Sydney wins to her total.

Laurie Morgan

Another interesting horse I trained at this time was Atlas, or more correctly, I trained a horse which had an interesting owner. Atlas was owned by Laurie Morgan, dual Olympic gold medalist and captain of Australia's first ever gold medal winning equestrian team at Rome Olympics in 1960. I had known Laurie long before I started training and before his Olympic triumphs. A group of us used to go each weekend to a mutual friend's property at Turramurra in Sydney where Laurie coached us in show jumping and cross country riding.

In 1981 he sent me Atlas, a strong 16.2 hands chestnut, to train.

Laurie was at the stables one afternoon, around 3pm, the time when horses are out for their afternoon walk, and he asked if it would be okay for him to ride Atlas out? Sure, why not.

I told him to follow others from the stable and do about 15 laps of the so called 'bull ring', an area on the racecourse just inside the Doncaster Avenue-High Street corner, where a circuit of about 200 metres caters for horses which are stabled in the 'half mile' area, to walk their afternoon exercise.

By 4pm all my horses, other than Atlas, had returned, but I was not concerned until a half-hour later, at which time the racecourse goes into lock-up for the night. There was no sign of Laurie and Atlas, so I walked out to look for them.

As I reached the end of the short lane from the stables, which links into the roadway which leads to the bullring, a nightwatchman was locking off the lane way to our back entrance. I told him there was one horse still out, so he said he would come back in 15 minutes.

With still no sign of Laurie and Atlas, I walked on until I was half way down the roadway. Then, there they were, walking toward me on a loose rein. Laurie said that as he had never seen the back area of the racecourse, he had gone for a ride up the hill area of what used to be the old steeplechase course behind the 1,200 metre start. Then he thought he had better follow my instructions and walk the 15 laps of the bull ring.

"You were lucky you didn't get locked into the bull ring; they lock there as well." I said.

"Oh I was," Laurie replied, "but I jumped out."

My reaction was shock. How could a racehorse jump a two metre high railing fence without a ground line! What Atlas jumped was equal to an obstacle used in A-Grade show jumping. Anybody who knows show jumping will understand what a challenging jump this was.

But then I realised. Laurie Morgan? Of course! Not only dual Olympic gold medalist, but the man who had followed up by competing (and finishing) in the 7.2 kilometre famous (or is it infamous?) 1962 Grand National steeplechase at Aintree in England. Also twice winner of the Fox Hunters' Cup over the same gruelling course. Silly me. Of course, any horse owned by Laurie Morgan would have been schooled to jump.

Two weeks later Atlas showed he could also gallop when he won his first city race for me.

Racing - The Great Leveller

$\sim$

Racing is known as the sport of kings - which it is. Both kings and queens have been regular participants for hundreds of years, but it is also the sport of a full cross section of the population.

It is also a great leveller.

I have seen some of the greatest brains of Australia, Macquarie street medical specialists, members of the judiciary, even a prime minister, hang on the words of a teenager strapper, then hurry off in the direction of the betting ring.

Some punters seem to think that anybody connected with a racing stable has inside information. To me inside information is a myth. In a race of say ten starters, maybe one trainer will be conservative and say, "I'm hoping," another may cautiously say their horse is an each way chance; three will say they have a great chance and five will declare their horse a certainty. Which one should be listened to? So much for inside information.

Racing has a wide attraction and through it I have met many prominent personalities. At a Canterbury mid-week meeting in 1983 I was in the enclosure after winning a race, and two committeemen came across with congratulations. There was another man with them whom they introduced. I missed out on his surname and only got his name as Jack. That was okay; he called me Betty, so I called him Jack. I vaguely thought I knew his face but he had an American accent so I assumed I was mistaken. He said he would like to see my horse which, while we were talking, had been led away by the strapper, so Jack, the committeemen and I, walked in a group to the tie-up stalls.

I was showing him my horse and making polite conversation and it came out that Jack was very involved in the horse world in America. He told me that he not only raced horses, but also bred them and also that he and his brother worked in helping handicapped kids to ride. After about five minutes, his committeemen hosts hinted that they return to the committee room, but Jack kept yakking about how some things were similar in our racing worlds and some things were different; he was telling me about the horses he had bred and asking about the breeding here. He gave no sign of leaving. Despite the committeemen obviously wanting their guest to move on, he stayed, and we talked for about half an hour. I was interested in his ideas on both differences and similarities in racing and breeding in our countries, and he was interested in what I told him about Australian ways.

Tiger had not been with us but had been close by and watching, so when Jack had gone, I asked Tiger, "Who was that?"

He replied, "Didn't you know? That's Jack Klugman." The name didn't immediately register with me until Tiger said, "You watch him on TV every week in The Odd Couple."

Oh! I then realised why he had stayed with me for so long. I was possibly one of the very few people who didn't bring the conversation around to his acting and television career.

Another day I won a race at Randwick when guests of

the club were the famous American basketballers, the Harlem Globetrotters, and the race had been named in their honour. After the race, a group of them were in the enclosure and of course, as the winning trainer, we were introduced. In conversation they said they would like to see my stables. Sure, no problem. So it was arranged and they visited the next day.

They were a joy to entertain, but I was concerned at the bad manners of my two apprentices of the time who were both 4feet 10inches (1.47metres) and who kept making remarks about the Globetrotters height, all over 6feet 6inches (1.98metres). But the Globetrotters were apparently accustomed to it and were equally amused by the smallness of the apprentices and were in disbelief that these little kids could ride and hold powerful racehorses.

All staff were photographed with them and all were given Globetrotters' autographs to show off to friends.

Innovations

When Tiger returned from the USA with his hearing he also returned with some new style racing gear - a full elastic girth and surcingle set. Until then, racing girths and surcingles were of webbing with an insert of about 20 centimetres of elastic, and it was not uncommon for a saddle to slip backwards (or sometimes work forward), on a galloping horse. The full length elastic, gripping over its full length, was a wonderful safety development. This was 1979 and they were being quickly adopted by American jockeys because of their anti-saddle slipping safety.

'Wow,' I thought, 'what a super idea'. Were we allowed to use them in races? No way. The authorities said they had not been tested, and they were barred! Just another brick wall I met in racing! Now, no jockey would ride in a race with anything other than full elastic.

Another first was introduced by one of my staff, Ian McIntyre, who had been to the Sydney Royal Easter Show, then held at nearby Moore Park, and brought home a headband of small flashing lights. For fun, he put it on his skullcap next morning and rode out. I liked it. It was much easier to pin point which was my horse on the other side of the track in the half light of pre-dawn training. He was told to get it off. Soon afterwards lights on skull caps became commonplace; different trainers with different coloured lights.

I was losing count of how many times I had been told "No" by authority! NO we don't license women. NO you cannot use full elastic girths and surcingles. NO you can't have lights on skull caps. NO we don't have girl apprentices. NO we don't register apprentices over 21 years of age. Who broke through these barriers? Me. Another NO I had been given was when I first moved to Randwick, when I suggested I keep my Geurie stable. Oh NO. At the time I was fearful of letting anything jeopardise my move to Randwick, so I didn't push it. Today satellite stables are commonplace.

I had always claimed that I got where I did without any help from the AJC, but in 1982 I did get wonderful help from them when told I had been advanced to a No.1 licence - the first woman in Australia. A No.1 licence was very special as trainers started on a Permit, then only if proving proficient, he/she (big progress! – the rule books had been changed to include 'she'), could be advanced to a No.2 trainer. Then, from around 1,300 trainers throughout New South Wales, only 20 to 30 made it to the prestige grade of a No 1 trainer. Since then, these gradings have been abolished.

Also, my ego was occasionally boosted if my name was listed in the top ten Sydney trainers. Once a week the daily newspapers used to publish a list of the current top ten trainers and their position in the Sydney premiership. In the 1980's my name was sometimes in the list; not often, and sometimes just scraping into 9th or 10th place, but after the obstructions I had met to reach this level, I felt I had made it.

In the 1984-85 season I was 14th in the Sydney Trainers' Premiership - not bad for a female with an average of 20 horses in work and up against 120 males.

Timothy

Nine from ten trainers, if asked which race they would most like to win, will answer, 'the Melbourne Cup'. For me it was the Golden Slipper, but I didn't do it. I had six runners and went close four times, but in racing, being close is not memorable; it is only winning that counts.

To qualify a horse to start in the Golden Slipper is, in itself, an achievement, as the field is decided by prize money earned. I did this six times, and all with inexpensive horses. There was Smokey Jack who finished a close second, Belle Tetue fourth, Timothy fourth and Kabul, Duke Diamond and Nibric's Hope - all good runs.

Timothy's fourth was a great effort in 1985. Up against the cream of breeding, against horses purchased for six-figure sums, Timothy was a budget priced yearling from a country sale ring. A brown colt by Merriville from Abbey Road, Tiger bought him as a yearling for $4,000 at a Dubbo sale in 1984. Within minutes he was claimed by one of our owners, Bill Eccleston of Trangie. This was fine as I had trained for Bill at Geurie and it was nice to have him re-join our Sydney stable.

Timothy's first win was at Warwick Farm in the John

Oxley Stakes, followed by winning the STC Skyline Stakes and the AJC Up and Coming Stakes. In the Slipper he ran a great fourth after copping interference near the finish.

After the Golden Slipper he went for a spell to Princes Farm at Hawkesbury, then owned by John Singleton. All was well until two months later when, on the day the float was booked to bring him back to stables, we had a phone call to say that when he was being led to be loaded on to the float, they found he was lame. No one knew what had happened. I said to load him anyway and bring him back to the stables and we would find out here what the problem was.

What we found out was that he had a cracked stifle. It was a serious problem and all credit to veterinarian John Peatfield who treated him and got him back to 100 per cent again. It was probably nobody's fault; unfortunately these things happen. It could have been a kick from another horse; he could have hit a fence; he could have fallen over and landed badly. Who knows? Horses seem to have a knack of being easily injured but John Singleton took the accident to heart.

It was certainly no fault of his but he felt responsible. When Timothy had recovered, John insisted on not only spelling him without charge, but he put him in the yard and stable which had been that of John's own champion horse, Strawberry Road, so that he could keep an eye on him.

After a lengthy spell Timothy came back to racing in 1987 and was back to winning form. It had been bad luck that he missed running in the important autumn three-year-old races which carry good prize money, but he did well as a four-year-old and won nine races during his career.

The only horse I ever trained that was a true Melbourne Cup prospect was Ponchielli. He had raced in New Zealand for one win before he came to me. Although on the small side, he had an enormous length of rein and could stay all day. After winning three times over the testing Randwick 2,400 metres and setting the course record, I set plans for the 1987 Melbourne Cup. But, no way could either Tiger or

I convince his owner that he was a Cup prospect. It was an unyielding 'No.'

Who knows? It was one of those things. The owner has the final say. But, I still feel he would have performed well in the Cup.

Kevin Langby and the Red Coat

I n the 1980's Kevin Langby owned a men's clothing store in Pitt Street, Sydney, though he took no part in the shop's operation, leaving all to a manager. One day, after he and Tiger had been to lunch in Chinatown, as the shop, named The Stable, was only two blocks away, Kevin thought to call in. When they left the shop Tiger was carrying a parcel, a present from Kevin, of a very bright cherry-red blazer jacket.

Tiger had always followed the correct dress code for the Members' enclosure at the races, but the following Saturday, when he appeared ready for the races, he was sporting the new bright red jacket.

I was not impressed. Appropriate attire for men in the Members' enclosure was either a suit, usually navy or grey, or occasionally some men wore a navy blazer with grey slacks. The only red jackets were worn by the clerks-of-the-course. I tried to bully Tiger out of wearing it, but threats fell on deaf ears. He said that as Kevin was riding one of my horses that day, it would seem ungrateful if he didn't.

So I said, "Stay away from me."

And he did. I think not because of what I had said; I think he knew himself that it was too much.

My horse was in a tight three-way finish and there was a delay as Kevin and the other two hopefuls stood waiting on the track until the photo was examined. They waited, as the winner has to lead the others in.

Just as the announcer called my horse the winner, Kevin dropped the reins on the horse's neck and jubilantly threw his arms in the air. As Kevin rarely showed emotion in racing, some spectators could have interpreted this as a great plunge brought off! No way. Simply coincidental. Simply that Kevin had spotted Tiger standing alone at the other end of the enclosure in the flashy red jacket!

I never found out, but have my suspicions that it had been a dare by Kevin and bravado by Tiger.

Lester Piggott

Rustglow, a big chestnut horse, had been a handy performer winning country races around the Gunnedah area before he came to me in 1983. I trained him for three years and he totalled 19 firsts.

One of his wins was in February 1985, in an Open Highweight handicap at Randwick, for which I had booked Mick Dittman for the ride. But, on the Wednesday before the races, I had a phone call from Tony King, then Chief Executive of the AJC. After pleasantries, Tony asked if I would give the ride on Rustglow to the renowned English jockey Lester Piggott. Tony explained that Lester was a special guest of the AJC; that he was doing a Grand Farewell tour of Australia; that he had ridden winners on all other major racetracks in Australia except Randwick. I told him I had booked Mick Dittman, who had won on Rustglow at his previous start, and if he was prepared to ask Mick to stand down, that it would be okay with me; but I was not going to be the one to do the asking.

Mick did agree. It would have been difficult for him to say, 'No,' to the AJC.

Much had been written in the press about Lester, quoting his lifelong ambition to ride a winner at Randwick. But, despite good rides throughout the day, by the time the last race came around the ambition was still unrealised and there were several despondent committeemen in the enclosure, seemingly resigned to accepting that Randwick was not going to record the hoped for win by the great international jockey.

Everybody happy that Lester Piggott had finally scored a Randwick win.

Then came the last race and Rustglow won by 1½ lengths. Suddenly I seemed to be the most popular trainer at Randwick. Smiles of relief were everywhere and I was invited 'upstairs', as the Committee Room is referred to, for drinks and to bring Tiger and Rustglow's owners with me.

When we were there, passing pleasantries and munching on nibblies, Lester Piggott's manager approached me with the suggestion that it is usual to give the great man an additional 5% of the prize money. Besides their riding fee, jockeys officially get 5% of the prize and are sometimes given extra as a bonus, but I thought any extra for Piggott was not warranted. It had been an easy ride; he had done none of Rustglow's track work leading up to the race, whereas Mick Dittman had, and he had been given the ride at Mick Dittman's loss, so I said, "Sorry. If anybody gets an extra 5% it will be Mick."

Also, Piggot had an easy ride as Rustglow was in good form. The following week he backed up again for another win at Randwick, this time winning by 6½ lengths and giving my 16-year old apprentice Craig Rixon his first ever city winner.

Colours

Often mistakenly referred to as 'silks', the shirt/jacket worn by jockeys are 'colours' and various combinations of colours are registered with racing authorities by owners for their sole use. If an owner does not have registered colours, it is usual to use the trainer's colours.

Silks are the riding breeches worn by jockeys, so named as before the days of synthetic fabrics they were made of silk (from silkworms), then the strongest lightweight material available.

My racing colours were, 'Pink, dark blue seams and cap' which had been trainer Reg Cook's colours when I had Delville Chief with him in 1962. When I went to the country, Reg gave me these colours as a present and transferred their registration to my name. It was a nice present - not because of the material value, but because they were a combination of only two colours - which was pretty near impossible to get. Thousands of racing colours combinations are registered, and to get a new individual set, it usually has to be a 'Jacob's coat, a hotch potch combination of four, possibly five different colours.

Many years later on a trip overseas, Tiger was at Singapore races and saw a horse racing in colours described in the race book as pink, but which were really bright cerise. He made enquiries, found the Singaporean tailor who specialised in racing colours, and brought me home a set of colours made up in this much brighter cerise. I used them for many years, but still registered as 'Pink, dark blue seams and cap'.

The Racing Calendar, a publication mailed monthly to trainers, gives information on race dates, programmes, barrier trials, jockey's contact phone numbers, special notices and such. Randwick trainers would get their copy a few days earlier than others, per courtesy of an AJC official who attended track work each morning to take nominations and acceptances from trainers, and who, each month, when the Calendar was published, brought the trainers' copies with him. From 6am to 7am he was in an improvised office in a shed near what was known as 'the half mile crossing', after which he went across to another office at 'the mile' from 7am to 8am, as a service for trainers who worked from that area.

One morning, having collected my Calendar early, I read that three new colours had been added to the official list - cerise, burgundy and fawn.

Although my colours were registered as 'Pink with dark blue seams', in a race the narrow blue seams blended into the bright cerise appearing as all cerise. Wow, wouldn't it be beaut I thought, to have the cerise officially. So I hurried around to the AJC office thinking that, if I delayed, somebody else would beat me to it.

I was told by the Racing Manager that 'All cerise' had been registered by popular committeeman Jack Ingham. Okay, my ego kicked in and I asked, "Well, how about the All burgundy?" It was pure vanity on my part as a solid colour suggests prestige, such colour sets usually having been held by a family since the start of registration. I was told they had also gone, so I asked for 'All fawn'.

"I don't know Betty, I'll check." The Racing Manager

went to another office for a few minutes then returned smiling, and said, "Yes, it's okay, they're yours."

After getting the all fawn colours I relinquished registration of the pink, dark blue seams and cap and legendary golfer Norman von Nida took them over.

Some years later, Tiger, who had no vanity about colours, and had always liked the pink combination, was talking to Norman and casually mentioned he had always preferred the original colours. Norman told Tiger that he no longer had a horse to race and if we would like them, he would transfer those colours back to Betty.

From then on I used the 'All Fawn' as my personal colours and the original set, now described as cerise instead of pink, for owners who had no registered colours of their own.

To some people colour is important, to others it is of no account. My mother would never back a horse carrying any green; in fact she would not wear anything to a race meeting with even a speck of green. One day she was at the races without a pencil and a friend offered her a green one. Thank you, but no thank you. She came home with an unmarked race book. To me, green has been lucky. My first Listed race win was in 1977 when Smokey Jack won The Breeders Plate and his colours were nothing but green - light green with dark green stars. So much for superstition.

Also, I lean to the opposite of most people's thinking about number 13. I had a lot of luck with 13- always pleased to collect my saddle from the Weighing Room and carry out the 13 saddle cloth.

Another thing which both Tiger and I liked, was to name horses with proper names - among them were Keith, Timothy, Nickson, Neville and Michael, so for one horse which was special to Tiger, when it came to giving him a name, it followed the pattern and became Wayne. Wayne was special to Tiger as, indirectly, the horse owed his life to Tiger.

At a Dubbo horse sale in 1984 Tiger spotted a mare, Ragtime lady, which I had trained some years earlier. When her turn came to be sold there was only one bidder and Tiger recognised him as a knackery buyer. So Tiger bid against him. Although Tiger used to make out he was tough, he was a softie and hated to see anything mistreated.

I was not at the sale and when he came home and told me he had bought Ragtime Lady because he thought she would be a good broodmare, I was, to say it politely - displeased. He knew my feelings on breeding. I prefer to go to a sale and buy a horse of choice instead of getting whatever happens to be born.

Instead of telling me he had wanted to save the mare's life, he had told me the porky about wanting to breed. But when he realised I was truly irked, he gave the true reason. What could I say? I understood. I felt the same way about the lovely gentle mare I had recently trained.

There is justice in life, and the reward came when Ragtime Lady produced a colt foal, Wayne, which, although not a top galloper, did win a race in Sydney and had provincial wins.

Buying at sales brought some very useful horses into the stable, particularly from Tasmania. which was always great value for money. For many years, David Yates of Kiama always had two or three useful horses with me – some were horses he had purchased as yearlings, some he had bred himself by the stallion, King Zavata, in Queensland. In 1985 he asked me to go with him to Launceston yearling sales. I did - though doubting it would be worthwhile. I had looked at the catalogue; knew none of the breeding, and thought there would be nothing worth buying.

I was very wrong. Breeding was not international standard, but several yearlings had nice conformation, which is my way of selection. We bought two yearlings and both were winners. From then on I went regularly to Launceston sales, held each February, to buy for other clients and always came home with one or two yearlings. Remarkably, every horse I bought there, won races. Not all were metropolitan winners, but not one missed out on being a winner. Some were top performers; among them Nickson, bought for $6,000 at Launceston. Among his important wins was the 1987 FJ Carberry Quality Handicap at Randwick, a Listed race in which he defeated Beau Zam (the horse which went on to be Australian Horse of the Year). Nickson was 100/1; Beau Zam was odds on. He then ran second to Beau Zam in the Spring Champion Stakes, a Group One race. Among Nickson's other wins was the Parramatta Cup in 1989. Not bad for $6,000.

Another bargain Launceston yearling sales buy was Koflach Valley, whose four wins also included a Parramatta Cup (1991). Expensive? No. $8,500. Launceston was great value for money.

I think this 100% success with Launceston buys, was a combination of the Tasmanian climate which is similar to that of two of the world's foremost breeding countries, Ireland and New Zealand, and to good conformation.

To me, conformation has always been the most important criterion. Never having big money to buy on breeding, I relied on looks. Many years before, I had trained myself in what to look for. Brought up with horses I knew the features and I knew the faults, and although I accepted this knowledge as being correct, years before starting out as a rookie trainer at Geurie, I looked for myself.

I used to go to the races at Randwick for the big carnival meetings, where top horses were racing, and as they paraded in the enclosure I would be glued to the fence trying to forget what I knew about conformation, searching to find what was common to the top horses. Most features were what I expected, but concentrated looking helped reinforce the overall picture of the different angles of joints, of length or shortness of various bones. Although there are differences in a stayer to a sprinter most features are common to good gallopers.

Judges of horses know that depth of girth and width of chest are indications of heart and lung space and veterinary surgeons are widely employed to do heart and lung assessments on horses for prospective buyers. Even though Davies Johnston was a good friend, I never imposed on him to check out a horse prior to sale day - simply because, limited by price, I never knew what I would be bidding on until the actual sale of a horse started.

It has always amused me when a person says they selected a horse because it had a nice head. I like a nice head, but other than width at the gullet suggesting plenty of room for the windpipe, and size of nostrils for breathing, the shape or look of the head is not high on my priorities. They don't gallop with their head.

Or, because the horse had a good kind eye. Maybe kind, maybe unkind; that the horse has two eyes with good eyesight is what matters about eyes. It is the angle of joints, length of bone, straightness of legs, size of chest area, the girth, and the power of the rump to look for.

Another successful horse, though not from Tasmania, that proved a bargain buy was Athelnoth at $5,000. At an Inglis' weanling sale, a colt by Coronation Day from Cloudcrest was walking around the parade yard behind the sale ring and caught my eye. I watched him walk down to be sold, and though I had not until then looked at his breeding, I bid. Vince Coles was at the sales and as soon as I had bought the weanling, Vince said he would like a share. This was ideal as he lived on acreage at Arcadia, which meant his property would be a good place for the youngster to finish growing. So, he was raced by Vince and his wife Lorraine, myself and Tiger and was trained by Tiger as I retired before Athelnoth raced. His nine wins included the Group 2 Royal Sovereign Stakes in 2003.

I, and then Tiger, trained for Vince for many years and we had several horses together and many winners. Another one of the good ones was a horse Vince had bred himself, Butterfly Star, winner of five races.

Sydney Staff

During my 15 years at Warbett Lodge stables at Randwick we had many loyal staff. As in most stables there are some strappers who drift in and out, but there are some who are dedicated and dependable. One was Claire Scivyer.

One afternoon a man and his 15 year old daughter knocked on the stable gate. He introduced himself as Ralph Scivyer and his daughter as Claire. She was leaving school and wanted to work with horses; she could not ride, she had no experience, but her keenness was so obvious that I thought she deserved a trial.

The trial developed into ten years and Claire proved to be one of the best strappers we could wish for. Her father was unbelievably supportive. For three years, until Claire turned 18 and able to have her own car, he drove her from their home at Botany, six kilometres, to be at stables by 4am, six days a week.

At the same time we had Hugh Moran, a very good rider, who was studying for the priesthood and living at the Catholic seminary at Kensington. Before joining the church he had been a stockman and prominent rodeo competitor but he was not a 'rough rider'; he was a top horseman with the gift of being able to settle horses. Hugh, who was with us for three years, had been given permission from the seminary to work part time each morning.

Another who was with us, on and off, for some years was Tiger's older brother Evan, known as Barry and later known as Rev. He was training at Rosehill and living in a caravan at the stables - despite having his own home in Clovelly. Tiger, concerned about him living at the stables, suggested he give up, that he come to work for us and would be able to live back in his own home.

Barry and I did not always see eye-to-eye, but he was kind to horses and to me that was a big plus. At the time he was in his sixties and had a troublesome knee, but if we had a problem horse he never hesitated to ride it - despite having to be helped on because of his knee. He had a calming effect, able to settle down fractious horses and ease the hardest of pullers.

When Barry came to work for us, Hugh was one of our regular track work riders, and Mick Stanley, the AJC's supervisor of morning track work, knowing Hugh was from the seminary, would respectfully address him as Brother. Then when Barry started to ride work, Mick heard Tiger referring to Barry as 'brother', something Tiger had done since they were little boys. Mick (wrongly) assumed Barry was also from the seminary and respectfully addressed him in the same way.

When riders from another stable overheard Mick's "Good morning Reverend," one of them burst out laughing, calling out, "He's no Brother," and the other rider's hooting reply came, "Perhaps he's a Reverend!" From this banter developed Barry's nickname, which for a while was Reverend, then shortened to Rev., and the name stuck.

Morning Stables

ℳ

It was once said o me, "Racing has been good to you." No way. It was hard work that was good to me; hard work brought success. But I give thanks that I was healthy and able to work.

Work started at 4am all mornings, except Sundays, when we started at 5am. Summer or winter was no different. First job of mine was to peek into each box for a quick check on each horse, then to the feed room to mix each horse's breakfast.

First job of Tiger's was to wake staff, who were occasionally (correction – very occasionally) up and about. Actually over the years we had really good, loyal staff, and that Tiger had to often wake them up was a very minor minus. Besides permanent staff, there were casuals who came in for five hours each morning to do yard work; mucking out (getting rid of overnight manure and topping up the bedding with fresh straw) in each box while the horse was out doing its training. They also saddled horses and hand walked them - so they would be warmed-up and ready for the riders. By the time everything got into routine, the first horses would be walking out the back gate to the track around 5am.

On a blackboard outside my office, I chalked the sequence in which each horse was to be saddled and hand walked for 20 minutes. As a rider returned on one horse after its track work, the next horse was ready, saddled and warmed up.

Yard staff would take over the returning horse, unsaddling and letting it loose in the sand roll for a few minutes. Sweaty and itchy from the saddle, and not having hands like us to scratch themselves with, horses loved rolling in sand. Then they were taken to the hosing dock to have the sand and sweat hosed off; then scraped of surplus water, towel dried as much as possible, then into their box which had been nicely cleaned, the straw bed fluffed up - with breakfast and clean water waiting.

Each morning I rode out on my taxi (pony Ickle), to 'my' spot on the inside of the tracks near the course's 2000 metre mark. Going to the same spot each morning and clocking gallops always from the same angle, is the way to get a line on each horse. All trainers have their own usual spot for the same reason.

The routine never changed. Horses could not be left in their boxes all day without exercise; so if there was torrential rain; bad luck - we got wet.

Now there is a tunnel entrance which goes under the tracks, but when I was training we got to the centre of the course by crossing over the tracks at the half-mile. In the centre is an ashes and metal circuit of about 1,000 metres, where horses trot around to warm up before going on to whichever track is being used that morning for their main work. One winter, when we had inches of rain daily for a week, and with hundreds of horses going in and out over the same narrow section of the crossing, the area was a bog. I could feel Ickle straining to pull his leg out after each step had sunk halfway up his shins in the quagmire.

Winter time was not much fun when bitterly cold

southerly gales, which always seemed to be strongest just before dawn, were blowing. I don't know if I was better off, or worse off, than the track work riders. I was bundled up with all sorts of winter underwear, thick wool jumper and down-filled trousers and parkha covered by a Drizabone oilskin coat. I was sitting on Ickle in the one spot; the riders were moving which to a degree would have warmed them (particularly if on a hard puller), but I think we were all the same – very cold.

But such mornings were balanced out on good weather mornings with some spectacular sunrises. Sydney City Council puts on an annual Light Show in the city with coloured lights playing on various major city buildings and landmarks, but such man made lighting effects are nothing to some of the light shows seen from the centre of Randwick racecourse at dawn. Within a few minutes of scarlet slivers imposing on a jet black sky the colour can change to blood red then to cerise, to bright pink, into orange then cream then disappear with full daylight. The transition of each colour lasts only a few minutes but it can be spectacular.

One morning in 1988 I was sitting on Ickle in my usual position in the centre of the track when I noticed three men in business suits standing together, about 20 metres from me. They had bowler hats and furled umbrellas. Most unusual. I thought they must be businessmen who had come to see their horse work, yet, even for businessmen they seemed to be extremely correct in their dress. It was intriguing, but none of my business.

Later it was the talk of the track.

And also, talk of the track, was Ron Quinton.

Princess Anne was in Sydney and it had been arranged for her to ride track work on Bart Cummings' outstanding horse of the year, Beau Zam. The well dressed men were her aides-cum-security men.

Being a very experienced rider, Princess Anne had no trouble in riding Beau Zam in its work, but seems she was not aware of Australian strict trackwork rules. All riders must obey the rule which states that a slower moving horse must move out from the rails and make room to let a horse that is galloping, to come through on the inside. Working alongside Princess Anne was retired jockey, Harold Light, on another Bart Cummings' horse; perhaps he was too well mannered to tell her what she should do. Seems Princess Anne's horse was going three-quarter pace and Ron Quinton was coming up behind them in full gallop. Ron is reported to have called out several times and when the rider in front of him didn't move over, he blasted the rider with a string of very expressive expletives!

Harold, who had been one of my regular jockeys for many years before he retired from race riding, told me that Princess Anne was completely unfazed by the language. Not so Ron Quinton. Seems that at the time he had no idea whom he was blasting and had to cop taunts for many weeks afterwards.

Another morning I remember well, was in September 1983. As soon as I awoke that morning I turned on the TV to get a quick update of the America's Cup yacht race before I went to the stables. With Australia II well in front and only a few kilometres to go, I wanted to keep watching. Australia seemed a living certainty. But as it is in horse racing, no win is certain until past the post. Half-an-hour later I was sitting on Ickle in the track centre, when the honking of horns, by seemingly every car in the neighbourhood, signalled the news. There was no mistaking the sudden euphoria - Australia had won the America's Cup.

I have been asked many times, "Why do horses get trained so early in the mornings?"

It goes back to the Second World War when manpower was needed for the war effort. Most strappers and track work riders had to work in a factory job starting at 7.30am, so to get their stable work done, it meant training had to start early. Throughout the war years trainers did little travelling. Petrol was rationed and certainly not available for horse transport, so trainers usually just raced their horses at meetings on their home track, often with only five races on the programme. Also, there was no mid-week racing. When war ended and racing picked up, and horses were able to travel, the race clubs programmed more races with earlier starts. Also, rules came in that horses had to be on the course one hour (later two hours), before their race time.

So, early training hours continued.

I Owe You

The wide front stable gates to Doncaster Avenue were only opened when a Kensington Produce Company truck was delivering our weekly supply of fodder. At all other times it was kept safely shut. Other trucks and horse floats used our back entrance which opened to the course. For people coming to the stables through the front entrance, there was a smaller gateway, big enough for people but not for horses. This was a safety measure so horses could not get out.

One early afternoon the front gates were opened for a fodder truck delivery which, parked in the entrance, seemingly blocked it. But, a strapper was about to hand lead a horse to go out the back for afternoon exercise, when, sudden drama. The horse pulled away and somehow was able to squeeze through the small gap at the side of the truck and was off into the street.

Panic! I rushed out to see said horse fast trotting along the centre of the roadway towards Centennial Park about 800 metres away. I knew I had little hope of catching him on foot, but my car was parked close by in the street, so I grabbed the keys and was in pursuit.

There are footpaths and cycle ways surrounding Centennial Park and, fortunately, when I caught up with the horse, he was there, head down, munching on the grass strip separating the paths. I stopped the car in a 'No Standing' area - only one thought was to catch the horse. He was a sensible horse, and having a bridle on was easy to catch..... but, what do I do now? How do I get both car and horse back?

I was trying to think what to do, when a voice said, "G'day Miss Lane. You okay?" It was one of Tom Smith's staff walking home from the city. Phew, I could breathe again. Help was here. It was Peter Moody, a young chap at the time, and he said "I'll take him back for you."

I thought Peter would lead the horse home, but without asking if the horse was quiet, he took the reins, threw them over the horse's head, vaulted on him bareback and walked off. I called out after him, "Thanks Peter, I owe you one."

That was over 30 years ago and I have never since spoken to Peter, the trainer of the great unbeaten Black Caviar.

I still owe him one.

William Street

When I was young my mother owned a Victorian style terrace house in William Street, Randwick built in 1888, which she had later sold.

Skimming through the local paper one day in 1988 I read an ad. that this house was to be auctioned on site at 1.30pm on the following Saturday. That was a Randwick race day and I had a runner in the first race and another in the fifth. As the auction timing fitted in nicely, I said to Tiger, "I'm going across to have a sticky-beak at the old house." The walk to William Street is only five minutes from the racecourse so, by going after the first race, I knew I could be back in plenty of time for the fifth.

I had gone only to look, no thoughts of buying, but when bidding lulled at what seemed well under value, on impulse, I put my hand up. In 1988 it was not necessary for bidders to pre-register. The house was in shabby disrepair and had not attracted buyers, and for a while there were no more bids. For a few minutes I thought I had bought it, then bidding picked up again. Two more bids against me, and the auctioneer said it had not reached the reserve: that it was being passed in.

This left me as the third highest under-bidder, but I just thought, 'Okay, that's that'.

I had to get back to the races to saddle up and was starting to leave, when, again on impulse, I said to the auctioneer, "I can't stay, but I am interested," and gave him by business card.

When I got back to the races Tiger must have had suspicions and queried, "You didn't buy it did you?"

"No," I assured him, "of course not."

Tiger had little interest in money and was never concerned how I managed our finances, but three days later the estate agent did contact me - and I did buy it, for a very reasonable price.

When Tiger first saw the house he was appalled and wanted nothing to do with it. It had obviously been used as a rooming house as each bedroom door had individual locks. What had been a pantry had been turned into a shower; the front sitting room had been used as another bedroom; worn linoleum was on the kitchen floor. The whole place was tatty and grubby. So, we left it as it was and let one of our staff live in it, as it was, rent free.

We were still living in the AJC house at 158 Doncaster Avenue, Kensington when a year later, Ian McIntyre, who had worked us many years earlier at Geurie, came to work for us again. He, and his partner Rose, needed a home in Sydney, so the solution suited perfectly. We would renovate William Street for ourselves and let Ian and Rose live in the AJC's house. I assumed that the attitude of the AJC of their house as being 'too good for staff' which had virtually forced me to live there, had been forgotten. And as I had paid their rent regularly, there was no hindrance.

It took two months to completely gut and renovate the old terrace - new plumbing, new wiring, new bathrooms, new kitchen, painting - everything. The makeover cost more than the house, but it was now comfortably livable and with a panoramic view across the racecourse, Tiger and I happily moved in and Ian and Rose moved into the house at the stables.

Happy Betty.

Women Accepted

D espite, by now, my full acceptance in racing as a No.1 trainer, and acceptance of a handful of other women trainers and jockeys, racing was still a male domain. Even as late as 1986, David Hickie produced a book, 'Gentlemen of the Australian Turf' - over 400 pages featuring men in racing. Seems women still did not rate enough to be acknowledged. In another publication of 750 pages, 'Australian Horse Racing 1988' on personalities in Australian racing, women totalled less than three pages. However, barriers had broken down;

Although I was still the one and only female trainer at Randwick, women trainers were licensed at Warwick Farm, Rosehill and Canterbury; females were riding in races, stables were employing male and females equally as stable hands and women finally had full AJC membership. There had been a movement in 1978 to admit women to AJC 'associate' membership, but it had been stymied by an injunction from one of the members. It took more years and much lobbying until, in 1982, an aware AJC committee held a meeting, changed the rules and full membership was offered to women.

Besides breaking through the barrier against female

trainers I broke another barrier when I signed up the first ever girl apprentice in Australia. Females riding in races had been treated as a novelty and referred to by the condescending title of 'jockettes' when a few progressive (or perhaps short of riders) picnic race clubs programmed races for females. Only a very occasional race for females was held at a registered meeting until pioneer Pam O'Neill and New Zealander Linda Jones broke down the barriers and were the first to ride equally against men. Pam's persistence in travelling extensively in Queensland and New South Wales, to wherever a picnic race meeting scheduled a ladies race, was rewarded when she became the first female to be licensed in Australia. Linda had broken down the barriers in New Zealand in 1978 when she was licensed there and in 1979 came to Australia, where she later set the standard by winning Queensland's Fourex Cup at Doomben in 1982.

Accepted as among the leading trainers when a group was flown to Scone Yearling sales. l to r: Darby Armstrong, Frank Penfold, Dave Sweeney, Pud Burton, Jack Denham, Geoff Chapman, John Page, Pat Murray and seated me and Neville Begg.

Australia's first ever officially licensed female apprentice, Joanne Clark, who came from neighbouring suburb Maroubra, had been working at Warbett Lodge as a stable hand for 12 months. She was keen to be apprenticed, so I approached the AJC. I was told that the subject of girls being apprenticed had been discussed, but as need for change had not come up, rules concerning apprentices were still "he". When I applied for Joanne, there was no objection, the issue was fast forwarded, rules amended, and in March 1979 Joanne became the first Australian female apprentice jockey. She had ridden ponies from age eight and after a year's hard work in the stable and with tuition from Tiger, she was ready, at age 17, for her first Barrier Trial ride to be assessed by the Stewards. Joanne passed easily and was ready for her next Trial when love called and she and our horse breaker, Ron 'Gogo' Fitzsimmons, left to be married and live in Newcastle.

I was, shall I say, 'not happy!' I was thinking of the general reaction from the AJC, of how it would affect the chances for other girls. But seems I was over reacting as from then on, girls were widely accepted. Joanne did continue her interest in racing when Gogo became a trainer and she worked for 15 years as his foreman (or should it be forewoman?) at Newcastle. Later, she went to the Sunshine Coast in Queensland and became a trainer herself.

Years ago I was quoted as saying I would be doubtful to put a girl on one of my horses in a race; my thoughts being that girls are every bit as good as guys in horsemanship - but their point of balance differs. Males in general, have a better point of balance with wider shoulders and narrower hips, whereas females generally have wider hips and narrower shoulders.

I am now happy to eat my words.

In 1979 I had a fully professional female jockey riding work for me, Irish 'jockette' (officially so-called in Ireland), Helen Maloney, was the first and only female professional jockey in Ireland at the time. She had gained her licence in

June that year after a four year apprenticeship, the same as boys, and had ridden four winners. She had come to Sydney to gain experience riding track work during the winter lull in Ireland's racing, In my opinion Helen was the equal of any of our leading jockeys and, had she been cleared to ride here, I certainly would have used her..

Some years later another girl, Bernadette Cooper, who mixed it equally with top jockeys in Sydney, reinforced my change of mind. She came from Queensland after being leading apprentice there, and rode winners for me in the 1990's. Not only a good rider, she could get off a horse and was accurate in judging its ability.

Apprentices

Besides breaking through for female apprentices, I wrangled another change when I indentured the first older aged apprentice. In 1980, school leaving age was 14 years and if a boy wanted to be a jockey, he left school then. Very few were apprenticed after turning 15 as, irrespective of when the apprenticeship commenced, it ended when they turned 21.

When an apprenticeship ended, so too did their claiming of a weight allowance in races - a major incentive for owners and trainers to give them race rides. It meant the younger a boy became apprenticed, the longer time he had to ride with the benefit of an allowance.

David Smith was 18 when he came to Warbett Lodge. Although his ambition was to be a jockey, his parents had thought otherwise, assuming that if he finished High school he would then take on what, to them, would be a more conservative career. When he passed the Leaving Certificate, they asked what career he would like to follow?

"I want to be a jockey."

Had he been apprenticed then, at age 18, he would have

had little chance of riding in a race with the benefit of an allowance. It could take up to two years for him to ride in the number of official Barrier Trials needed to get approval to ride in races, and by then he would be 21 - no longer eligible for an allowance.

L to r: Karen Godfrey, Stephen Ratten, Maurice Logue, Tiger, me, Lance Donnelly, David Smith and Debbie McClelland. The four boys were all apprenticed and all rode winners.

I pointed out to the AJC that times were changing, that the school leaving age had risen, and that present day education was not only desired, but necessary. They agreed. Rules were changed and David was approved, age 19, as the first senior aged apprentice. Four years were then set as the term of indenture, with a race riding allowance of three kilograms until the apprentice had ridden 20 winners, two kilograms up to 50 winners and 1.5 kilograms up to 80 winners. Provision was also made for an extension of four years in special circumstances - such as an apprentice losing time through injuries or illness.

David lived up to our Warbett Lodge tradition of first race ride being a winner. He did this at a Kembla Grange meeting, then doubled in his second race ride with another win, this time at Canterbury.

At this time we had another apprentice, the only one who didn't follow our pattern of first race ride to be a winner. He didn't follow the pattern simply because he was already a successful Randwick apprentice before he transferred to me from Theo Green in 1981. Maurice Logue had finished second to Wayne Harris in the Sydney apprentices' premiership in the previous season, but glandular fever had then put him out of racing for six months. When Maurice's health improved and he was able to resume riding, Theo had a full complement of apprentices and by racing's rules could not take him back.

When Theo asked if I would take over Maurice's apprenticeship, I was delighted. Tiger and Maurice's father, Ian 'Doc' Logue, who had also been a jockey, had been mates from their own apprenticeship days and Tiger was Maurice's godfather. I had first met Maurice when Tiger took me to meet Doc and his wife, Leslie, at their home in Dubbo, soon after I arrived in the area in 1962. Maurice would not remember it - he was 12 months old.

He had not long started an apprenticeship at Orange when his father was tragically killed in a truck accident. Sympathetically, racing officials arranged for him to be apprenticed to Theo Green at Randwick. At the time, Tiger had been disappointed that Maurice had not come to us, but it was understandable - Theo was an outstanding teacher of apprentices.

Though not his first winner, Maurice's first win for me was memorable. It was on Chessington at Canterbury, and as he slid from the horse after the win, he said to me, "Thanks for the birthday present." It was his 19th birthday and he thought I had planned it. Instead of smiling and saying "Thank you," I admitted I had not realised it was his birthday - but I was very pleased it happened that way.

A short time before this, in October 1981, we had celebrated another birthday win, also unknown to me until after the win. In a tight finish in the Tiny Tots Stakes at Rosehill, between my horse Duke Diamond and owner-trainer Norm Williamson's horse, Sovereign Glory, Norm was standing next to me in the enclosure, waiting for the photo and said, "It will be a birthday present if my horse wins; today's my birthday."

But we got the verdict and when Duke Diamond was announced the winner, my owner, Bruce Paton, who had overheard Norm, said, "That's okay, it's still a birthday win. It's my birthday today too."

Tiger Takes Over

After 15 years of being the only woman trainer at Randwick, I retired in 1991. During my time there was only one other woman trainer there for a short period, Maureen Dittman, wife of jockey Mick Dittman, who when they moved from Brisbane to Sydney in 1984 brought two horses with her. Mick was one of my main race jockeys and I had come to know he and Maureen as friends, so I let her use two of my boxes for a short time until they got themselves settled. Later they bought a house with stables in Kensington and Maureen then trained from there. When the Dittmans moved back to Brisbane, I was again the only woman at headquarters.I had been training for 30 years and Tiger had been my support all that time. After he retired from race riding, he had been foreman for ten years, always accepting my control and I felt it only fair to give him a chance to train himself. Although we were married, I had stuck to the name Lane, with Tiger variously referred to by the press as my friend, partner, foreman, associate. Now it was his turn. Also, after 30 years of 365 days a year, the thought of taking things easier was appealing.

The Illawarra Turf Club honoured me at their final race meeting of the 1991 season. They had 'Farewell Betty' flashing on the Kembla Grange Totalisator Board between races; they named the main race the 'Betty Lane Farewell Handicap' and made a presentation to me. I was very touched.

Presentation at Kembla races on my retirement

By now, several women were training on both metropolitan and provincial tracks - successful trainers like Barbara Joseph, Kim Moore, Helen Page, Leslie Picken, and it was only a few months after I retired that the all-conquering Gai Waterhouse gained her licence. Nobody admires Gai more than I do. Saying she is the most successful female trainer in the world (which she is) may be well intentioned, but drop the adjective 'female'. She should not be put into a separate sub-category. She is one of the great trainers of the world - full stop. I unlocked the door for women; It could be said that Gai then opened it wide. No way. She didn't just open the door wide. She pushed it right off its hinges.

As Tiger wanted a smaller stable, the AJC allowed us to swap my complex of 22 boxes at 158 Doncaster Avenue, for smaller premises of ten boxes, which Pat Webster was then occupying three doors up the street, at 152 Doncaster Avenue. Years earlier these had been Harry Darwon's stables, later,

Jim Greenwood's. We knew the stables from years before in the 1970's when I had brought horses to Sydney to race and Jim had always made a box available for me.

Both complexes were similar in all but size. Both had direct entry from the street and direct access to the racecourse from the rear; both had spacious lofts for storage; both had staff accommodation; both had sand rolls; but a big plus was that we no longer had to rent the house which went with 158 Doncaster Avenue. In the changeover we transferred the 'Warbett Lodge - founded 1962' sign, (which we had brought with us from Geurie) and for 15 years had been at the entrance to 158 Doncaster Avenue, to Tiger's stables. It was now his.

He got off to a great start. His first winner was a black type race, the Parramatta Cup at Rosehill in January 1991 with Koflach Valley. He jokingly said that as I had won this race two years earlier with Nickson, he wasn't to be outdone.

Tiger had supported me and now I supported him. Who said you can't have your cake and eat it too? I was able to retire, but still keep my interest. Tiger trained the horses, I did the nominations and office work - but I no longer had to be out of bed every morning at 3.30am and at the stables by 4am. Sometimes, but not often, if he was short staffed I would fill in at morning stables to help saddle up, sometimes do the feeds, perhaps treat an injury to a horse, but I enjoyed not having the responsibilities and I enjoyed sleeping-in ; that is, if getting up at 4.30am instead of 3.30am can be called sleeping-in. A life-long habit of getting up early is hard to change.

Tiger used to joke that some afternoons I would walk into the stables unannounced and say, "This is wrong, that is wrong. Why isn't such and such done?" Then having stirred everybody up, I would leave. He said that staff still respected my position and when I left they would be scurrying around to do what I had said.

I had joined the Woollahra-Darling Point branch of the

Red Cross in 1988 and I was now able to give more time to this. I also had time to go to lunch with friends and I started Bridge lessons.

My pony, Ickle, was getting old when I retired and I gave him to my nephew, David Coates and his wife Vicki for his then, three-year-old daughter Olivia, to ride. At the time the family lived at Londonderry, but soon afterwards they moved to Brisbane and in the move Ickle went with them. They cared for him as I had. David and Vicki took four days to drive to Brisbane. Concerned that the trip would be hard on the old pony, they stopped every two hours to take him off the float for a leg stretch and rest.

After Tiger had been training for nearly a year we bought another pony, a 14 hands grey which Tiger named Matey, after Matey Molloy, a jockey friend of his from when they had ridden together in the country. But the 10 boxes of Tiger's stables were needed for racehorses and, as Matey was too big for makeshift accommodation such as Ickle had lived in at 158, the AJC allowed Matey to live in one of the stables, with its own yard, in the block used for the clerk-of-the-course greys. This was in another section of the racecourse about 200 metres away.

A friend, Don, who worked at Flemington fruit markets, used to come to us on Fridays, bringing two 30kgs sacks of carrots for the horses. Naturally, we took some up to Matey. When his next door neighbour, retired glamour horse Ming Dynasty, winner of 17 races including two Caulfield cups, then chief Clerk-of-the Course horse, saw Matey munching carrots, his head was over the rail whinnying. Thereafter, Ming and Matey shared a carrot party every Friday afternoon.

In Tiger's first year of training, September 1992, he came home very distressed one morning after barrier trials at Randwick. He had booked jockey Noel Barker to ride his horse but seems there had been a misunderstanding and Noel's name was also written down for another horse in the same Trial. Tiger had been the first trainer to engage Noel, but as the other trainer wanted Noel, Tiger said his was not important and he would get another jockey.

Fatal decision.

Pity that Tiger had not been selfish and had held Noel to the ride. Noel was killed in that Trial when a seagull caused his horse to fall. It brought back brought memories of when my horse Henderson had lost a race at Rosehill when hit on the cheek by a seagull. At the time I had been disappointed but it was only losing a race - something trainers become accustomed to - and not a tragic result like this.

Noel had only recently returned home to Randwick from Hong Kong, after winning the jockey's premiership there, and had brought presents for friends. For Tiger and me they were caps to wear over our skull caps at track work. Many track work riders' caps are 'borrowed' (seldom returned), from somebody's set of racing colours, but Noel's caps were special. He had thoughtfully remembered that Tiger followed the then Rugby League team, Balmain (colours red and black) and Tiger's present was a cap of red and black quarters in waterproof material. Mine, an attractive iridescent pale blue silk. Years later in 2007, when Tiger retired and we closed the stables and dispersed our racing gear, I kept very little - but I kept those two caps.

While on the subject of caps - in winter we used to wear woollen beanies over our skull caps to be pulled down at the back to keep one's neck warm, (or more correctly - to keep one's neck from not being quite as cold). For some time Tiger had been wearing a yellow and black beanie which he lost, so I went to a so-called 'two-dollar' shop for a replacement. I bought a red and white beanie this time, which must have been too big as on his second day of wear he came back to stables from the track minus beanie. Okay, I bought another one. This time I thought that the red, white and blue looked nice.

Tiger had been wearing it for a few mornings and was trotting his horse around the centre of the track, which is done as a warm-up before the horse's actual work, when another rider, Bobby Pearse, a loyal Eastern Suburbs Rugby League fan, caught up to him and said, "You're a nice turncoat. Do you change your team to whoever's leading?"

Tiger didn't have a clue what he was talking about; nor did I when Tiger told me about it later. I had no idea the beanies were in Rugby League football colours; nor any idea that it was just after Balmain (yellow and black as was Tiger's first lost beanie), had lost a match that I unknowingly decked him out in the St George Dragon's colours (red and white) who had won; then the following week in East's colours (red, white and blue) after they had won A case of unknowingly changing teams at the drop of a hat!

Three years after being licensed, Tiger was raised to a No.1 trainer and continued until health forced him to call it a day, in 2007.

Around the year 2000 he developed a gradually worsening swallowing problem with food and liquid going to his lungs, instead of his stomach. As there was no cure, doctors inserted a tube through his side directly into his stomach, through which he was fed five times a day, with prepared tinned nourishment. Although he had most of his feeding at home, we set up a section of the stable office into a hygienic area with a small bar fridge for his cans of 'food'.

He continued the daily routine of training, going to the stables each morning and each afternoon but it became difficult for him to attend race meetings, other than locally at Randwick, because of this five times a day feeding routine which had to be under strict hygienic conditions. I had been helping out at the stables, staying in the background, but when he could no longer go to race meetings, I resumed doing the races - saddling up, instructing jockeys and such. I had been his deputy for over three years; walking in and out of restricted areas; known and recognised by most officials in racing, never queried, until, at a Rosehill meeting in 2004, when I went to walk through the gate to the horse stalls to check on our horse, the woman on the gate asked to see my badge.

I said, "I don't have one. I'm Betty Lane. I'm saddling up for my husband, trainer Tiger Holland."

"You need a badge."

I repeated, "I don't have one."

"You can't come in."

I politely told her I needed to come in; that I had to check on my horse and that, also, I would be coming back later to saddle up.

"No you won't ; if you don't have a badge you won't be coming in."

I arrogantly thought, 'Oh yes I will,' and headed off to the racecourse office. I knew all the staff, (or thought I did), but being mid-afternoon they were out and about doing other jobs around the course, with only a new girl, whom I did not know, and who did not know me, alone in the office.

I said that I needed a ticket to enter the horse stalls. She said she had no authority to give me one, but, no doubt sensing my mood, suggested I see the racecourse detectives. Their office was nearby and fortunately both were there. I just barged in as, by this time, I was really riled. I told them the problem; told them if I couldn't go into the horse stalls area I would have the strapper lead the horse out and I would saddle it up in the public area.

"Calm down Betty, calm down. We'll come with you."

We walked the 200 metres back to the horse stalls, me raving, they still saying, "Calm down."

They politely told the lady gate keeper that, even though I had no badge, she was to allow me to come and go as I required. I glared at her; she glared at me.

When I came back later with the saddle and she had to open the gate for me, I smiled smugly and simpered, "Thank you."

The detectives who had stayed in the area, were seemingly

amused by it all and suggested that, to save future problems, I should consider registering as the stable foreman.

My arrogant reaction was, "What! Do you realise what you are suggesting?" Did they expect me to be a foreman after being a No1 trainer?

But I realised rules had to be followed, and as I was now retired I had no official position. Tiger's need for me was necessary for him to continue - and far more important than my ego. So I registered as stable foreman.

Training partnerships, which would have been the perfect a solution, were not allowed in Sydney until 2008.

Bridge Player

Next to the weighing scales outside the Jockeys' Room on Randwick racecourse there used to be a special entertaining room where winning connections were invited for celebratory drinks and 'nibblies' and to watch, then be given, the video of their win. I was deputising for Tiger when, after a win in early 1996, I was enjoying the club's hospitality, when AJC chairman, Tony Allport's wife, Margaret, came in and joined us. She apologized for being slightly late, explaining that she had been playing Bridge.

I thought no more about it until a week later when my club in the city announced they were starting a monthly Bridge competition within the club. I had begun Bridge lessons only a few months earlier and was keen, but I had a problem; I had no partner. When I remembered that Margaret Allport played bridge, the solution came to me. I could invite her as my guest.

I phoned and she said she would love to come. She came. We played. We finished last! I later wondered how she had put up with me! She was a State competition player and I, a beginner, who didn't know enough to realize how little I knew.

But we became good friends and she helped and coached me, playing Bridge as my partner and putting up with my mistakes. I did improve (gradually) and we sometimes won. Then for years we played together at each other's homes with mutual friends Dola Hines, Kay O'Sullivan and Christine Fay. The Allport's main home was in Queanbeyan, but, as they spent more time in Sydney than Canberra, when husband Tony needed to spend a lot of time at the AJC's office, they had bought what she referred to as their 'beach home', one house back from the cliffs at Coogee.

Some years later Margaret knew she had terminal cancer and, knowing she would die, had organised her own funeral. Although she died in Canberra, she had planned her funeral service at St Nicholas' Anglican Church, Coogee. Two days after she died, Tony came to my home and told me that she had asked for me to read the poem, 'Footprints in the Sand', at her funeral service, which I did. He had it printed out ready.

Few people in racing had known of our close friendship and there were many surprised people when I did the reading.

Margaret was some person.

Au Revoir Tiger

Tiger's swallowing problem had been gradually worsening and when he won a race with Athelnoth at Randwick in June 2006, and he could not make the short walk across the lawn to the winner's enclosure, I suggested he retire. He had walked part of the track the previous day which had exhausted him. But if Tiger's health was not good, it was a different story with his determination. "Not yet. I'm okay," he said.

He carried on for another year, on time every morning to the stables, back each afternoon, but by August, 2007, he had to give in. It was a hard decision, but incredibly it was made at the right time. I think somebody 'up high' was looking after him.

In August 2007, exactly one week after horses had left and we had closed the stable, a sudden disastrous equine influenza epidemic hit the Sydney horse world. Randwick racecourse went into immediate lock-down with a complete embargo on the movement of horses, and a quarantine which lasted from August 2007 until February 2008.

I shudder to think how we could have handled having a

stable full of horses, not allowed to do any track work; not even allowed out of their confined stable area for six months! All movement was absolutely prohibited. I do know that Tiger was not well enough to handle it, but I also know he would have tried, and that I would have come back to work full time. I also know that the work would have been treble that of normal, as horses would have needed much longer hand walking up and down the confined yard to keep them from foundering.

Tiger died in 2008, at which time he had had no food or drink whatsoever by mouth for six years - yet despite this, he had kept training, kept getting up at 3.30am every morning, kept driving himself to the stables until one year before he died.

If he could, Tiger always tried to make things easy for me. I jokingly say that, as he died on June 30, the exact end of the financial year, and as everything was in joint names, true to form, Tiger had made it simple for me for legal transfers and taxation.

His funeral at St Jude's church, Randwick, was packed and he was buried in the cemetery there. It is an old cemetery which has been closed for many years except to regular parishioners, which Tiger was. Sadly, the day of his funeral happened to be our wedding anniversary. We had married July 4, 1972; he was buried July 4, 2008. As this date is that of the USA's Independence Day, he used to joke that it should be re-named Loss of Independence Day.

When he died I lost my husband, my partner in racing, but more significantly, I lost my best friend.

Life After Training

~

In 30 years of training I was never suspended, never fined. I trained over 1,000 winners which at the time was believed to be the highest number of winners by a woman worldwide. However, with the great increase in the number of present day women trainers, this has been bettered. I achieved practically everything I set out to do. But the one thing I never achieved, was to be accepted equally as 'a' racehorse trainer, instead of female trainer, lady trainer or woman trainer. It always seemed there had to be a limiting adjective to separate me, to put me into a sub-group. I had set out to prove that I could train, which I did, so, remembering the discrimination of the times, perhaps I should be pleased that I achieved as much as I did.

In 1988 I received the Bi-Centennial Year Lady Sarah Kennedy award for the woman who had made the greatest contribution to racing in New South Wales; then in 2007 I was awarded an Order of Australia Medal in the Queen's Birthday Honours list for the same reason. Aside from racing, in 1988 I was awarded a Long Service medal from the Australian Red Cross for my work as president of the Woollahra-Darling Point branch.

Receiving the Bi-Centennial award for the woman who had made the greatest contribution to racing

My life is now very different to the full-on lifestyle I had for 45 years (30 as a trainer and 15 as a back-up for Tiger), when long hours left little time for anything else. I have caught up on interests which were put on hold for all those years. I have resumed painting; I teach drawing at my club in the city; I edit the Gazette journal for St Jude's Church, Randwick; I play Bridge; I belong to a group who walk in Centennial Park.

I have always been early to bed, early to rise. As a kid I used to be up early, either going for a swim at Coogee beach or riding my pony in Centennial Park before school and, after keeping racehorse trainer's hours for more than half a lifetime, I have not changed. Friends know not to phone after 7pm.

I have been asked many times that if I had my time over, would I do it again? As the trailblazer I made sacrifices; but I made them freely. There are few greater thrills than winning a race, whether it is a country Maiden or a city Group race, but it is a roller coaster life style. There are exciting successes - there are massive disappointments. Do I regret those early years of hardship? I had no choice. It was the life I had to accept as there was no other way of doing what I wanted to.

But? Would I do it again?

That would depend. Would it be under the same conditions or under today's conditions?

Apart from gender acceptance, the training world has changed. In my grandfather's time the average trainer had two or three horses in stables behind his home. In my era, a Randwick stable averaged 20 to 30 horses. Now there are many stables with more than 100 horses in full training with a back-up of hundreds more being either broken-in, pre-trained or spelling and several stables with over a hundred nominations in major races such as the Golden Slipper and the Derbies.

Training can be likened to what were once family run grocery stores on suburban street corners, to the multi-nationals Coles, Woolworths and Aldi. Racing is now international with horses flying around the world to race and jockeys flying to places like Hong Kong for one ride.

In my time, the usual pattern of becoming a trainer was growing up with a pony, working in stables as a strapper, progressing to becoming a foreman, then to trainer. Or, as a jockey who when either age or weight caught up, turned to training. Although these are still typical ways to racehorse training, now there are TAFE colleges which run courses for aspiring trainers who can qualify for a Diploma in Racing.

I have seen the development of women in racing, the improvement of attitude to women, and now, finally, complete acceptance. Would I do it again? It is a hypothetical question as today's circumstances are so very different. Although training is a full-on commitment, there is no comparison with the industry today to what it was when I started.

Would I do it again? I don't know.

Who I Am

I was born, Betty Denice Coates, at home, in Duke Street, Kensington, an eighth generation Aussie descended from three ancestors who came to Botany Bay on the First Fleet: James Bloodsworth, convict, later pardoned, who went on to build the first Government House; and who, when he died was given a State funeral; Sarah Bellamy, convict; and James Lee, marine. I grew up in Randwick. When I was 10 months old we moved to a newly built house in Eurimbla Avenue. My parents bought this house as it was in a cul-de-sac which they felt would be a safe street for my brother and me to play. My brother, Errol Joseph Coates, was four years older than me.

I discovered my genealogy when friend, Helen Carpenter, whose mother had died at her birth and whose father had died when she was eight, and who knew nothing of her ancestry, asked me to come with her to do research at the Genealogical Society in Sydney. I only went along to keep her company, but found my pedigree was all there.

I had been brought up to believe that Dad's family were very superior and my mother's family were working class. Dad's family (but never Dad himself) had a manner of superiority over my mother's family. But I discovered that my mother's family were all free settlers and Dad's family descended from convicts! It was quite a hoot. Until my trip to the Genealogical Society, when I was in my twenties, I had known none of this. At first I thought Dad must have kept this knowledge from me, but it is more likely he had known nothing of it himself. It would have been kept from him.

My grandfather, Dad''s father, Joseph Coates, who gained medals for mathematics and classics at the University of London, came to Australia in 1864 to take up a position as the Maths Master at Newington College, Sydney, and he went on to be headmaster at Fort Street High school; then back to be headmaster at Newington; then was appointed inaugural headmaster of the newly founded Sydney High School in 1883. He was a leading cricketer, captaining New South Wales and playing 32 matches against other 'colonies', (as Australian states were known as, prior to Federation), and in the Colonials team against a visiting English team (before the days of such contests being known as The Ashes). As a bowler he introduced the style known as a 'Yorker' - so named after him as he came from Yorkshire. He was a founder of the New South Wales Cricket Association and a life member of the Sydney Cricket ground.

Dad went to Newington College, became school captain and rowed for Newington in the inter-schools Head-of-the-River regatta, captained both their number one Rugby and cricket teams. Strangely, I knew none of these things which Dad had achieved until many, many years later. He served in the First World War and perhaps it was from an experience there that he blocked out all his past. I had a sort of idea that Dad had been a soldier but he had never spoken of it until one evening when I was about eight or nine when with my brother Errol, Mum and Dad we were sitting around the fire. Mum was the only industrious one with knitting needles click-clacking which must have so worked on my father's memories that he could not contain what he must have subdued for many years. "Do you know that your mother's knitting saved my life?"

It was the first time he had spoken of war, and I never knew him to speak of it again. Dad never went to any reunions, never went to the Anzac day marches. Except for what he told us that evening, I would have doubted he had ever been a soldier. He told us that he was sitting in the trenches in France with six others when another soldier friend who had just come off guard duty, joined them. Although his ground sheeet-cum-cape had kept his body relatively dry, his feet were saturated. Seems Dad said, "I got a parcel from my fiancee today of warm hand knitted socks. I'll go and get you a pair." When he returned they were all dead. A direct shell had hit.

My mother's ancestors settled in the Bathurst district in the mid 1800's. Her mother, Alice Maud Townsend, was from a farming family; her father, James Frost Mutton was a butcher boy to his father before riding in races and then becoming a racehorse trainer.

In the days of big families my mother was an only child. She was an outstanding rider winning Ladies High Jump events at the Sydney Royal Easter show, also won Ladies Trotting races there. I think I developed a type of complex as a kid from being told by friends and relatives that I would never be as good a rider as my mother - which was true. I was a reasonably good rider, but no way would I have ever faced up to the type of jumps which I have photos of her riding over. In her day, jumping events at Sydney Royal had solid obstacles. A jump referred to as 'the log fence' was exactly that - a 1.5 metres high bank of solid logs, each about 60 centimetres through. No flimsy plywood logs then.

My brother Errol had the same interests when growing up as I did. He was a good rider, winning several One and Three Day events and was in the finals for selection in the equestrian team that was the first ever to represent Australia in Olympic Games. It was when Melbourne held the Olympics in 1956 that, due to our inflexible restrictions which required any horse coming into Australia to have six months quarantine pre-arrival, the equestrian events were transferred to Stockholm in Sweden. In the final wash-up for the team Errol was named as first reserve, to be flown to Stockholm if anything befell a member of the team. Nothing befell anybody.

He was also a leading amateur rider at picnic race meetings in country New South Wales and used to joke that at one time he headed the Sydney Jockeys' premiership, which he actually did - for four days. Up until the 1970's the first race on the programme of the first meeting at Randwick of each new season (which begins on August 1, was the Corinthian handicap for amateur riders. In fact it was the one and only race each year at Randwick for amateur riders. When Errol won this race it placed him at the top of the Sydney Jockeys' premiership. Then, when the second race of the day was run and won, he still shared the premiership with that jockey. At the end of the meeting he could still claim to be leading the Sydney Jockeys' premiership (but sharing it with professional jockeys who also ridden one winner each that day). Thus he was equal leader until the following race meeting when a jockey riding two winners took the lead.

I went to Randwick Public primary school and so did Errol. He went on to the selective Sydney High school, but I continued high school at Randwick. My cousins all went to private schools, but I guess my mother's money priorities were for us to have our ponies and horses.

In those days Randwick public school ended after Third year (year 9) when we sat for what was then the Intermediate Certificate. I passed, no problem, with four A's and three B's, which was quite surprising as I now realise I was quite irresponsible and never studied. Education was not nearly as available as it is now and for me to continue school would have meant going to the nearest girls High school which was at Strathfield - per three changes of tram and train. So I left school.

As my birthday is 24 January, and as I was 14 when

I passed, I can truthfully say I left school at 14; or I can say I left school at 15, as that is the age I would have been when the new school year started. Or I could say that I left at 17, because after fiddling around uselessly, riding and swimming for six months, I was sent off to Business College to learn typing and shorthand. In those days girls either became nurses (which had no appeal to me), worked as shop assistants (I was never strong on being subservient), became school teachers (too much study for me) or office work (not keen - but it was the last choice). As I started business college half way through the year, then did another full course the next year I was seventeen when I finished.

Although my mother did not keep me at school, she never hesitated if I wanted to learn something. She used to say, "Knowledge is no load to carry," and I went through phases (all short) - learning to play the banjo mandolin, Latin, acting, art, photography, jitterbugging, all the time riding and swimming and being useless, until one day, Dad phoned home from work, for me to come to his office. Next week I was working. He had organised for me to start in the office of the printing branch of WD & HO Wills where he was a director. It was there I met Roger Lane, my first husband, and I married a year later - far too young.

Errol and I both studied art as kids, and both continued at it. From age 12 until I left school, Dad had taken Errol and me weekly to the city for private lessons from Oscar Brock, a well known artist of the time. Errol started his working life in the art department of the Glass Works in Moore Park, Sydney, but when the war had been going a few years, he turned 18 and joined the army. He served in New Guinea. After discharge he studied Interior Decorating at Sydney Technical College which later became TAFE and then UTS (University of Technical Studies) at Ultimo in Sydney. He later became head of this same Interior Decorating department.

Throughout my life I have done drawing and painting spasmodically. Maybe serious for a few years, then nothing for a few years, then back to it again. I am reasonably average, but no way near the artist my brother was.

Errol and I were always close; he was a great brother. He died in 2008, three months after Tiger. He and Tiger were my two great loves. I have no children.

Printed in the United States
By Bookmasters